D0064071

Smith Wigglesworth on

HEALING

Smith Wigglesworth on

HEALING

SMITH WIGGLESWORTH

 Whitaker House

Whitaker House gratefully acknowledges and thanks Glenn Gohr and the entire staff of the Assemblies of God Archives in Springfield, Missouri, for graciously assisting us in compiling Smith Wigglesworth's works for publication in this book.

Unless otherwise indicated, all Scripture quotations are taken from the *New King James Version*, © 1979, 1980, 1982 by Thomas Nelson, Inc. Used by permission. All rights reserved.

Scripture quotations marked (KJV) are taken from the *King James Version* of the Holy Bible.

SMITH WIGGLESWORTH ON HEALING

ISBN: 0-88368-426-8
Printed in the United States of America
Copyright © 1999 by Whitaker House

Whitaker House
30 Hunt Valley Circle
New Kensington, PA 15068

Library of Congress Cataloging-in-Publication Data

Wigglesworth, Smith, 1859–1947.
    Smith Wigglesworth on healing / by Smith Wigglesworth.
       p.   cm.
    ISBN 0-88368-426-8 (trade paper : alk. paper)
    1. Spiritual healing—Sermons. 2. Pentecostal churches—Sermons.
3. Sermons, English. I. Title.
    BT732.5.W495   1999
    234'.131—dc21   98-54803

2 3 4 5 6 7 8 9 10 11 12 13 / 11 10 09 08 07 06 05 04 03 02 01 00 99

Contents

Introduction

n encounter with Smith Wigglesworth was an unforgettable experience. This seems to be the universal reaction of all who knew him or heard him speak. Smith Wigglesworth was a simple yet remarkable man who was used in an extraordinary way by our extraordinary God. He had a contagious and inspiring faith. Under his ministry, thousands of people came to salvation, committed themselves to a deeper faith in Christ, received the baptism in the Holy Spirit, and were miraculously healed. The power that brought these kinds of results was the presence of the Holy Spirit, who filled Smith Wigglesworth and used him in bringing the good news of the Gospel to people all over the world. Wigglesworth gave glory to God for everything that was accomplished through his ministry, and he wanted people to understand his work only in this context, because his sole desire was that people would see Jesus and not himself.

Smith Wigglesworth was born in England in 1859. Immediately after his conversion as a boy, he had a concern for the salvation of others and won people to Christ, including his mother. Even so, as a young man, he could not express himself well enough to give a testimony in church, much less preach a sermon. Wigglesworth said that his mother had the same difficulty in expressing herself that he did. This family trait, coupled with the fact that he had no formal education because he began working twelve hours a day at the age of seven to help support the family, contributed to Wigglesworth's awkward speaking style. He became a plumber by trade, yet he continued to devote himself to winning many people to Christ on an individual basis.

In 1882, he married Polly Featherstone, a vivacious young woman who loved God and had a gift of preaching and evangelism. It was she who taught him to read and who became his closest confidant and strongest supporter. They both had compassion for the poor and needy in their community, and they opened a mission, at which Polly preached. Significantly, people were miraculously healed when Wigglesworth prayed for them.

In 1907, Wigglesworth's circumstances changed dramatically when, at the age of forty-eight, he was baptized in the Holy Spirit. Suddenly, he had a new power that enabled him to preach, and even his wife was amazed at the transformation. This was the beginning of what became a worldwide evangelistic and healing ministry that reached thousands. He eventually ministered in the United States, Australia, South Africa, and all over Europe. His ministry extended up to the time of his death in 1947.

Several emphases in Smith Wigglesworth's life and ministry characterize him: a genuine, deep compassion for the unsaved and sick; an unflinching belief in the Word of God; a desire that Christ should increase and he should decrease (John 3:30); a belief that he was called to exhort people to enlarge their faith and trust in God; an emphasis on the baptism in the Holy Spirit with the manifestation of the gifts of the Spirit as in the early church; and a belief in complete healing for everyone of all sickness.

Smith Wigglesworth was called "The Apostle of Faith" because absolute trust in God was a constant theme of both his life and his messages. In his meetings, he would quote passages from the Word of God and lead lively singing to help build people's faith and encourage them to act on it. He emphasized belief in the fact that God could do the impossible. He had great faith in what God could do, and God did great things through him.

Wigglesworth's unorthodox methods were often questioned. As a person, Wigglesworth was reportedly courteous, kind, and gentle. However, he became forceful when dealing with the Devil, whom he believed caused all sickness. Wigglesworth said the reason he spoke bluntly and acted forcefully with people was that he knew he needed to get their attention so they could focus on God. He also had such anger toward the Devil and sickness that he acted in a seemingly rough way. When he prayed for people to be healed, he would often hit or punch them at the place of their problem or illness. Yet, no one was hurt by this startling treatment. Instead, they were remarkably healed. When he was asked why he treated people in this manner, he said that he was not hitting the people but that he was hitting the Devil. He believed that Satan should never be treated gently or allowed to get away with anything. About twenty people were reportedly raised from the dead after he prayed for them. Wigglesworth himself was healed of appendicitis and kidney stones, after which his personality softened and he was more gentle with those who came to him for prayer for healing. His abrupt manner in ministering may be attributed to the fact that he was very serious about his calling and got down to business quickly.

Although Wigglesworth believed in complete healing, he encountered illnesses and deaths that were difficult to understand. These included the deaths of his wife and son, his daughter's lifelong deafness, and his own battles with kidney stones and sciatica.

He often seemed paradoxical: compassionate but forceful, blunt but gentle, a well-dressed gentleman whose speech was often ungrammatical or confusing. However, he loved God with everything he had, he was steadfastly committed to God and to His Word, and he didn't rest until he saw God move in the lives of those who needed Him.

In 1936, Smith Wigglesworth prophesied about what we now know as the charismatic movement. He accurately predicted that the established mainline denominations would experience revival and the gifts of the Spirit in a way that would surpass even the Pentecostal movement. Wigglesworth did not live to see the renewal, but as an evangelist and prophet with a remarkable healing ministry, he had a tremendous influence on both the Pentecostal and charismatic movements, and his example and influence on believers is felt to this day.

Without the power of God that was so obviously present in his life and ministry, we might not be reading transcripts of his sermons, for his spoken messages were often disjointed and ungrammatical.

However, true gems of spiritual insight shine through them because of the revelation he received through the Holy Spirit. It was his life of complete devotion and belief in God and his reliance on the Holy Spirit that brought the life-changing power of God into his messages.

As you read this book, it is important to remember that Wigglesworth's works span a period of several decades, from the early 1900s to the 1940s. They were originally presented as spoken rather than written messages, and necessarily retain some of the flavor of a church service or prayer meeting. Some of the messages were Bible studies that Wigglesworth led at various conferences. At his meetings, he would often speak in tongues and give the interpretation, and these messages have been included as well. Because of Wigglesworth's unique style, the sermons and Bible studies in this book have been edited for clarity, and archaic expressions that would be unfamiliar to modern readers have been updated.

In conclusion, we hope that as you read these words of Smith Wigglesworth, you will truly sense his complete trust and unwavering faith in God and take to heart one of his favorite sayings: "Only believe!"

One

The Power of the Name

ll things are possible through the name of Jesus (Matt. 19:26). *"God also has highly exalted Him and given Him the name which is above every name, that at the name of Jesus every knee should bow"* (Phil. 2:9–10). There is power to overcome everything in the world through the name of Jesus. I am looking forward to a wonderful union through the name of Jesus. *"There is no other name under heaven given among men by which we must be saved"* (Acts 4:12).

Speaking the Name of Jesus

I want to instill in you the power, the virtue, and the glory of that name. Six people went into the house of a sick man to pray for him. He was a leader in the Episcopal Church, and he lay in his bed utterly helpless. He had read a little tract about healing and had heard about people praying for the sick. So he sent for these friends, who, he thought, could pray *"the prayer of faith"* (James 5:15). He was anointed according to James 5:14, but because he had no immediate manifestation of healing, he wept bitterly. The six people walked out of the room, somewhat crestfallen to see the man lying there in an unchanged condition.

When they were outside, one of the six said, "There is one thing we could have done. I wish you would all go back with me and try it." They all went back and got together in a group. This brother said, "Let us whisper the name of Jesus." At first, when they whispered this worthy name, nothing seemed to happen. But as they continued to whisper "Jesus! Jesus! Jesus!" the power began to fall. As they saw that God was beginning to work, their faith and joy increased, and they whispered the name louder and louder. As they did so, the man rose from his bed and dressed himself. The secret was just this: those six people had gotten their eyes off the sick man and were taken up with the Lord Jesus Himself. Their faith grasped the power in His name. Oh, if people would only appreciate the power in this name, there is no telling what would happen.

I know that through His name and through the power of His name we have access to God. The very face of Jesus fills the whole place with glory. All over the world there are people magnifying that name, and oh, what a joy it is for me to utter it.

Raising Lazarus

One day I went up onto a mountain to pray. I had a wonderful day. It was one of the mountains of Wales. I had heard of one man going up onto this mountain to pray and the Spirit of the Lord meeting him so wonderfully that his face shone like that of an angel when he returned. Everyone in the village was talking about it. As I went up onto this mountain and spent the day in the presence of the Lord, His wonderful power seemed to envelop and saturate and fill me.

Two years before this time, there had come to our house two lads from Wales. They were just ordinary lads, but they became very zealous for God. They came to our mission and saw some of the works of God. They said to me, "We would not be surprised if the Lord brings you down to Wales to raise our Lazarus." They explained that the leader of their church was a man who had spent his days working in a tin mine and his nights preaching, and the result was that he had collapsed and contracted tuberculosis. For four years he had been a helpless invalid, having to be fed with a spoon.

When I was up on that mountaintop, I was reminded of the Transfiguration (see Matthew 17:1–8), and I felt that the Lord's only purpose in taking us into the glory was to prepare us for greater usefulness in the valley.

> *An Interpretation of Tongues:* "The living God has chosen us for His divine inheritance, and He it is who is preparing us for our ministry, that it may be of God and not of man."

As I was on the mountaintop that day, the Lord said to me, "I want you to go and raise Lazarus." I told the brother who had accompanied me about this, and when we got down to the valley, I wrote a postcard. It read, "When I was up on the mountain praying today, God told me that I was to go and raise Lazarus." I addressed the postcard to the man whose name had been given to me by the two lads. When we arrived at the place, we went to the man to whom I had addressed the postcard. He looked at me and asked, "Did you send this?" "Yes," I replied. He said, "Do you think we believe in this? Here, take it." And he threw it at me.

The man called a servant and said, "Take this man and show him Lazarus." Then he said to me, "The moment you see him, you will be ready to go home. Nothing will keep you here." Everything he said was true from the natural standpoint. The man was helpless. He was nothing but a mass of bones with skin stretched over them. There was no life to be seen. Everything in him spoke of decay.

I said to him, "Will you shout? You remember that at Jericho the people shouted while the walls were still up. God has a similar victory for you if you will only believe." But I could not get him to believe. There was not an atom of faith there. He had made up his mind not to have anything.

It is a blessed thing to learn that God's Word can never fail. Never listen to human plans. God can work mightily when you persist in believing Him in spite of discouragement from the human standpoint. When I got back to the man to whom I had sent the postcard, he asked, "Are you ready to go now?" I replied, "I am not moved by what I see. I am moved only by what I believe. I know this: no man looks at the circumstances if he believes. No man relies on his feelings if he believes. The man who believes God has his request. Every man who comes into the Pentecostal condition can laugh at all things and believe God."

There is something in the Pentecostal work that is different from anything else in the world. Somehow, in Pentecost you know that God is a reality. Wherever the Holy Spirit has right-of-way, the gifts of the Spirit will be in manifestation. Where these gifts are never in manifestation, I question whether He is present. Pentecostal people are spoiled for anything other than Pentecostal meetings. We want none of the entertainments that other churches are offering. When God comes in, He entertains us Himself. We are entertained by the King of Kings and Lord of Lords! Oh, it is wonderful.

There were difficult conditions in that Welsh village, and it seemed impossible to get the people to believe. "Ready to go home?" I was asked. But a man and a woman there asked us to come and stay with them. I said to the people, "I want to know how many of you people can pray." No one wanted to pray. I asked if I could get seven people to pray for the poor man's deliverance. I said to the two people we were to stay with, "I will count on you two, and there is my friend and myself. We need three others." I told the people that I trusted that some of them would awaken to their privilege and come in the morning and join us in prayer for the raising of Lazarus. It will never do to give way to human opinions. If God says a thing, you have to believe it.

I told the people that I would not eat anything that night. When I got to bed, it seemed as if the Devil tried to place on me everything that he had placed on that poor man on the sickbed. When I awoke in the middle of the night, I had a cough and all the weakness of a man with tuberculosis. I rolled out of bed onto the floor and cried out to God to deliver me from the power of the Devil. I shouted loud enough to wake everybody in the house, but nobody was disturbed. God gave the victory, and I got back into bed again as free as I had ever been in my life. At five o'clock the Lord awakened me and said to me, "Don't break bread until you break it around My table." At six o'clock He gave me these words: *"And I will raise him up"* (John 6:40). I elbowed the fellow who was sleeping in the same room. He said, "Ugh!" I elbowed him again and said, "Do you hear? The Lord says that He will raise him up."

At eight o'clock they said to me, "Have a little refreshment." But I have found prayer and fasting the greatest joy, and you will always find it so when you are led by God. When we went to the house where Lazarus lived, there were eight of us altogether. No one can prove to me that God does not always answer prayer. He always does more than that. He always gives *"exceedingly abundantly above all that we ask or think"* (Eph. 3:20).

I will never forget how the power of God fell on us as we went into that sick man's room. Oh, it was lovely! As we made a circle around the bed, I got one brother to hold the sick man's hand on one side, and I held the other, and we each held the hand of the person next to us. I said, "We are not going to pray; we are just going to use the name of Jesus." We all knelt down and whispered that one word, "Jesus! Jesus! Jesus!" The power of God fell, and then it lifted. Five times the power of God fell, and then it remained. But the man in the bed was unmoved. Two years previously, someone had come along and had tried to raise him up, and the Devil had used his lack of success as a means of discouraging Lazarus. I said, "I don't care what the Devil says. If God says He will raise you up, it must be so. Forget everything else except what God says about Jesus."

A sixth time the power fell, and the sick man's lips began moving, and the tears began to fall. I said to him, "The power of God is here; it is yours to accept it." He said, "I have been bitter in my heart, and I know I have grieved the Spirit of God. Here I am, helpless. I cannot lift my hands or even lift a spoon to my mouth." I said, "Repent, and God will hear you." He repented and cried out, "O God, let this be to Your glory." As he said this, the power of the Lord went right through him.

I have asked the Lord to let me never tell this story except the way it happened, for I realize that God can never bless exaggerations. As we again said "Jesus! Jesus! Jesus!" the bed shook, and the man shook. I said to the people who were with me, "You can all go downstairs now. This is all God. I'm not going to assist him." I sat and watched that man get up and dress himself. We sang the doxology as he walked down the steps. I said to him, "Now tell what has happened."

It was soon told everywhere that Lazarus had been raised up. The people came from Llanelli and all the district around to see him and to hear his testimony. God brought salvation to many. Right out in the open air, this man told what God had done, and as a result, many were convicted and converted. All this occurred through the name of Jesus, *"through faith in His name"* (Acts 3:16). Yes, the faith that is by Him gave this sick man perfect soundness in the presence of them all.

A Lame Man Healed

Let us read a passage from the book of Acts:

Now Peter and John went up together to the temple at the hour of prayer, the ninth hour. And a certain man lame from his mother's womb was carried, whom they laid daily at the gate of the temple which is called Beautiful, to ask alms from those who entered the temple; who, seeing Peter and John about to go into the temple, asked for alms. And fixing his eyes on him, with John, Peter said, "Look at us." So he gave them his attention, expecting to receive something from them. Then Peter said, "Silver and gold I do not have, but what I do have I give you: In the name of Jesus Christ of Nazareth, rise up and walk." And he took him by the right hand and lifted him up, and immediately his feet and ankle bones received strength. So he, leaping up, stood and walked and entered the temple with them; walking, leaping, and praising God. And all the people saw him walking and praising God. Then they knew that it was he who sat begging alms at the Beautiful Gate of the temple; and they were filled with wonder and amazement at what had happened to him. Now as the lame man who was healed held on to Peter and John, all the people ran together to them in the porch which is called Solomon's, greatly amazed. So when Peter saw it, he responded to the people: "Men of Israel, why do you marvel at this? Or why look so intently at us, as though by our own power or godliness we had made this man walk? The God of Abraham, Isaac, and Jacob, the God of our fathers, glorified His Servant Jesus, whom you delivered up and denied in the presence of Pilate, when he was determined to let Him go. But you denied the Holy One and the Just, and asked for a murderer to be granted to you, and killed the Prince of life, whom God raised from the dead, of which we are witnesses. And His name, through faith in His name, has made this man strong, whom you see and know. Yes, the faith which comes through Him has given him this perfect soundness in the presence of you all."

(Acts 3:1–16)

Peter and John were helpless and uneducated. They had no college education; they had only some training in fishing. But they had been with Jesus. To them had come a wonderful revelation of the power of the name of Jesus. They had handed out the bread and fish after Jesus had multiplied them. They had sat at the table with Him, and John had often gazed into His face. Jesus often had had to rebuke Peter, but He had manifested His love to him through it all. Yes, He loved Peter, the wayward one. Oh, He's a loving Savior! I have been wayward and stubborn. I had an unmanageable temper at one time, but how patient He has been. I am here to tell you that there is power in Jesus and in His wondrous name to transform anyone, to heal anyone.

If only you will see Him as God's Lamb, as God's beloved Son, upon whom was laid *"the iniquity of us all"* (Isa. 53:6). If only you will see that Jesus paid the whole price for our redemption so that we might

21

be free. Then you can enter into your purchased inheritance of salvation, of life, and of power.

Poor Peter and John! They had no money. I don't think there is a person in this building as poor as Peter and John were. But they had faith; they had the power of the Holy Spirit; they had God. You can have God even though you have nothing else. Even if you have lost your character, you can have God. I have seen the worst men saved by the power of God.

Dealing with a Potential Murderer

I was preaching one day about the name of Jesus, and there was a man leaning against a lamppost, listening. He needed the lamppost to enable him to stay on his feet. We had finished our open-air meeting, and the man was still leaning against the lamppost. I asked him, "Are you sick?" He showed me his hand, and I saw that inside his coat he had a silver-handled dagger. He told me that he had been on his way to kill his unfaithful wife but that he had heard me speaking about the power of the name of Jesus and could not get away. He said that he felt just helpless. I said, "Kneel down." There on the square, with people passing back and forth, he got saved.

I took him to my home and clothed him with a new suit. I saw that there was something in that man that God could use. He said to me the next morning, "God has revealed Jesus to me. I see that all has been laid upon Jesus." I lent him some money, and he soon got together a wonderful little home. His faithless wife was living with another man, but he invited her back to the home that he had prepared for her. She came. Where enmity and hatred had been before, the whole situation was transformed by love. God made that man a minister wherever he went. Everywhere there is power in the name of Jesus. God can *"save to the uttermost"* (Heb. 7:25).

An "Incurable" Man Healed

There comes to mind a meeting we had in Stockholm that I will always remember. There was a home for incurables there, and one of the patients was brought to the meeting. He had palsy and was shaking all over. He stood up in front of three thousand people and came to the platform, supported by two others. The power of God fell on him as I anointed him in the name of Jesus. The moment I touched him, he dropped his crutch and began to walk in the name of Jesus. He walked down the steps and around that great building in view of all the people. There is nothing that our God cannot do. He will do everything if you will dare to believe.

Two

He Himself Took Our Infirmities

And He cast out the spirits with a word, and healed all who were sick, that it might be fulfilled which was spoken by Isaiah the prophet, saying: "He Himself took our infirmities and bore our sicknesses."
—Matthew 8:16–17

ere we have a wonderful word. All of the Word is wonderful. This blessed Book brings such life, health, peace, and abundance that we should never be poor anymore. This Book is my heavenly bank. I find everything I want in it. I desire to show you how rich you may be, so that in everything you can be enriched in Christ Jesus (1 Cor. 1:5). For you He has *"abundance of grace and...the gift of righteousness"* (Rom. 5:17), and through His abundant grace *"all things are possible"* (Matt. 19:26). I want to show you that you can be a living branch of the living Vine, Christ Jesus, and that it is your privilege to be, right here in this world, what He is. John told us, *"As He is, so are we in this world"* (1 John 4:17). Not that we are anything in ourselves, but Christ within us is our All in All.

The Lord Jesus is always wanting to show forth His grace and love in order to draw us to Himself. God is willing to do things, to manifest His Word, and to let us know a measure of the mind of our God in this day and hour.

A Leper Is Miraculously Cleansed

Today there are many needy ones, many afflicted ones, but I do not think anyone present is half as bad as this first case that we read of in Matthew 8:

> *When He had come down from the mountain, great multitudes followed Him. And behold, a leper came and worshiped Him, saying, "Lord, if You are willing, You can make me clean." Then Jesus put out His hand and touched him, saying, "I am willing; be cleansed." Immediately his leprosy was cleansed. And Jesus said to him, "See that you tell no one; but go your way, show yourself to the priest, and offer the gift that Moses commanded, as a testimony to them."* (Matt. 8:1–4)

This man was a leper. You may be suffering from tuberculosis, cancer, or other things, but God will show forth His perfect cleansing, His perfect healing, if you have a living faith in Christ. He is a wonderful Jesus.

This leper must have been told about Jesus. How much is missed because people are not constantly telling what Jesus will do in our day. Probably someone had come to that leper and said, "Jesus can heal you." So he was filled with expectation as he saw the Lord coming down the mountainside. Lepers were not allowed to come within reach of people; they were shut out as unclean. Ordinarily, it would have been very difficult for him to get near because of the crowd that surrounded Jesus. But as Jesus came down from the mountain, He met the leper; He came to the leper.

Oh, leprosy is a terrible disease! There was no help for him, humanly speaking, but nothing is too hard for Jesus. The man cried, *"Lord, if You are willing, You can make me clean"* (Matt. 8:2). Was Jesus willing? You will never find Jesus missing an opportunity to do good. You will find that He is always more willing to work than we are to give Him an opportunity to work. The trouble is that we do not come to Him; we do not ask Him for what He is more than willing to give.

"Then Jesus put out His hand and touched him, saying, 'I am willing; be cleansed.' Immediately his leprosy was cleansed" (v. 3). I like that. If you are definite with Him, you will never go away disappointed. The divine life will flow into you, and instantaneously you will be delivered. This Jesus is just the same today, and He says to you, *"I am willing; be cleansed."* He has an overflowing cup for you, a fullness of life. He will meet you in your absolute helplessness. All things are possible if you will only believe (Mark 9:23). God has a real plan. It is very simple: just come to Jesus. You will find Him just the same as He was in days of old (Heb. 13:8).

Jesus Heals by Saying a Word

The next case we have in Matthew 8 is that of the centurion coming and pleading with Jesus on behalf of his servant, who was paralyzed and was dreadfully tormented.

> *Now when Jesus had entered Capernaum, a centurion came to Him, pleading with Him, saying, "Lord, my servant is lying at home paralyzed, dreadfully tormented." And Jesus said to him, "I will come and heal him." The centurion answered and said, "Lord, I am not worthy that You should come under my roof. But only speak a word, and my servant will be healed. For I also am a man under authority, having soldiers under me. And I say to this one, 'Go,' and he goes; and to another, 'Come,' and he comes; and to my servant, 'Do this,' and he does it." When Jesus heard it, He marveled, and said to those who followed, "Assuredly, I say to you, I have not found such great faith, not even in Israel! And I say to you that many will come from east and west, and sit down with Abraham, Isaac, and Jacob in the kingdom of heaven. But the sons of the kingdom will be cast out into outer darkness. There will be weeping and gnashing of teeth." Then Jesus said to the centurion, "Go your way; and as you have believed, so let it be done for you." And his servant was healed that same hour.*
> (Matt. 8:5–13)

This man was so earnest that he came seeking Jesus. Notice that there is one thing certain: there is no such thing as seeking without finding. *"He who seeks finds"* (Matt. 7:8). Listen to the gracious words of Jesus: *"I will come and heal him"* (Matt. 8:7).

In most places where I go, there are many people whom I cannot pray for. In some places there are two or three hundred people who would like me to visit them, but I am not able to do so. Yet I am glad that the Lord Jesus is always willing to come and heal. He longs to help the sick ones. He loves to heal them of their afflictions. The Lord is healing many people today by means of handkerchiefs, even as He did in the days of Paul. (See Acts 19:11–12.)

A woman came to me in the city of Liverpool and said, "I would like you to help me by joining me in prayer. My husband is a drunkard and every night comes into the home under the influence of drink. Won't you join me in prayer for him?" I asked the woman, "Do you have a handkerchief?" She took out a handkerchief, and I prayed over it and told her to lay it on the pillow of the drunken man. He came home that night and laid his head on the pillow in which this handkerchief was tucked. He laid his head on more than the pillow that night, for he laid his head on the promise of God. In Mark 11:24, we read, *"Whatever things you ask when you pray, believe that you receive them, and you will have them."*

The next morning the man got up and, going into the first saloon that he had to pass on his way to work, ordered some beer. He tasted it and said to the bartender, "You put some poison in this beer." He could not drink it and went on to the next saloon and ordered some more beer. He tasted it and said to the man behind the counter, "You put some poison in this beer. I believe you folks have plotted to poison me." The bartender was indignant at being charged with this crime. The man said, "I will go somewhere else." He went to another saloon, and the same thing happened as in the two previous saloons. He made such a fuss that he was thrown out.

After he left work that evening, he went to another saloon to get some beer, and again he thought the bartender was trying to poison him. Again, he made such a disturbance that he was thrown out. He went to his home and told his wife what had happened and said, "It seems as though all the fellows have agreed to poison me." His wife said to him, "Can't you see the hand of the Lord in this, that He is making you dislike the stuff that has been your ruin?" This word brought conviction to the man's heart, and he came to the meeting and got saved. The Lord still has power to set the captives free.

Jesus was willing to go and heal the sick servant, but the centurion said, *"Lord, I am not worthy that You should come under my roof. But only speak a word, and my servant will be healed"* (Matt. 8:8). Jesus was delighted with this expression and *"said to the centurion, 'Go your way; and as you have believed, so let it be done for you.' And his servant was healed that same hour"* (v. 13).

Facing a Demon-Possessed Woman

I received a telegram once urging me to visit a case about two hundred miles from my home. As I went to this place, I met the father and mother and found them brokenhearted. They led me up a staircase to a room, and I saw a young woman on the floor. Five men were holding her down. She was a frail young woman, but the power in her was greater than the strength of all those young men. As I went into the room, the evil powers looked out of her eyes, and they used her lips, saying, "We are many; you can't cast us out." I said, "Jesus can."

Jesus is equal to every occasion. He is waiting for an opportunity to bless. He is ready for every opportunity to deliver souls. When we receive Jesus, the following verse is true of us: *"Greater is he that is in* [us], *than he that is in the world"* (1 John 4:4 KJV). He is greater than all the powers of darkness. No man can meet the Devil in his own strength, but any man filled with the knowledge of Jesus, filled with His presence, filled with His power, is more than a match for the powers of darkness. God has called us to be *"more than conquerors through Him who loved us"* (Rom. 8:37).

The living Word is able to destroy satanic forces. There is power in the name of Jesus. My desire is that every window on the street have the name of Jesus written on it.

Through faith in His name, deliverance was brought to this poor bound soul, and thirty-seven demons came out, giving their names as they came forth. The dear woman was completely delivered, and the family was able to give her back her child. That night there was heaven in that home, and the father, mother, son, and his wife were all united in glorifying Christ for His infinite grace. The next morning we had a gracious time in the breaking of bread.

All things are wonderful with our wonderful Jesus. If you would dare rest your all upon Him, things would take place, and He would change the whole situation. In a moment, through the name of Jesus, a new order of things can be brought in.

In the world, new diseases are always surfacing, and the doctors cannot identify them. A doctor said to me, "The science of medicine is in its infancy, and we doctors really have no confidence in our medicine. We are always experimenting." But the man of God does not experiment. He knows, or ought to know, redemption in its fullness. He knows, or ought to know, the mightiness of the Lord Jesus Christ. He is not, or should not, be moved by outward observation but should get a divine revelation of the mightiness of the name of Jesus and the power of His blood. If we exercise our faith in the Lord Jesus Christ, He will come forth and get glory over all the powers of darkness.

Christ Bore Our Sickness and Sin

When evening had come, they brought to Him many who were demon-possessed. And He cast out the spirits with a word, and healed all who were sick, that it might be fulfilled which was spoken by Isaiah the prophet, saying: "He Himself took our infirmities and bore our sicknesses."   *(Matt. 8:16–17)*

The work is done if you only believe it. It is done. *"He Himself took our infirmities and bore our sicknesses."* If only you can see the Lamb of God going to Calvary! He took our flesh so that He could take upon Himself the full burden of all our sin and all the consequences of sin. There on the cross of Calvary, the results of sin were also dealt with.

*Inasmuch then as the children have partaken
of flesh and blood, He Himself likewise shared
in the same, that through death He might destroy him who had the power of death, that is,
the devil, and release those who through fear
of death were all their lifetime subject to bondage.*   *(Heb. 2:14–15)*

Through His death there is deliverance for you today.

Three

The Confidence That We Have in Him

*Now this is the confidence that we have in
Him, that if we ask anything according to His will,
He hears us. And if we know that He hears us,
whatever we ask, we know that we have the
petitions that we have asked of Him.*
—1 John 5:14–15

t is necessary to discover the meaning of these wonderful verses. There is nothing that will bring you such confidence as a life that is well pleasing to God. When Daniel's life pleased God, he could ask to be protected in the lions' den. But you cannot ask with confidence until there is a perfect union between you and God, as there was always a perfect union between God and Jesus. The foundation is confidence in and loyalty to God.

Obtain the Confidence That Christ Had

Some people think that when Jesus wept after Lazarus's death, his tears were due to the love that

33

He had for Lazarus. But that was not the reason. Actually, He cried because He knew that the people who were around the grave, even Martha, had not come to the realization that whatever He would ask of the Father, the Father would give to Him. Their unbelief brought brokenness and sadness to the heart of Jesus, and He wept.

The moment you pray, you find that the heavens are opened. If you have to wait for the heavens to be opened, something is wrong. I tell you, what makes us lose confidence is disobedience to God and His laws.

At Lazarus's graveside, Jesus said that it was because of those who stood there that He prayed but that He knew that His Father always heard Him (John 11:42). And because He knew that His Father always heard Him, He knew that the dead could come forth.

There are times when there seems to be a stone wall in front of us. There are times when there are no feelings. There are times when everything seems as black as midnight, and there is nothing left but confidence in God. What you must do is have the devotion and confidence to believe that He will not fail, and cannot fail. You will never get anywhere if you depend on your feelings. There is something a thousand times better than feelings, and it is the powerful Word of God. There is a divine revelation within you that came when you were born from above, and this is real faith. To be born into the new kingdom is to be born into a new faith.

How to Be Useful to God

Paul spoke of two classes of Christians, one of which is obedient, and the other disobedient. The obedient always obey God when He first speaks. It is these people of God whom He will use to make the world know that there is a God.

You cannot talk about things that you have never experienced. It seems to me that God has a process of training us. You cannot take people into the depths of God unless you have been broken yourself. I have been broken and broken and broken. Praise God, for *"the LORD is near to those who have a broken heart"* (Ps. 34:18). You must have a brokenness to get into the depths of God.

There is a rest of faith; there is a faith that rests in confidence on God. God's promises never fail. *"Faith comes by hearing, and hearing by the word of God"* (Rom. 10:17). The Word of God can create an irresistible faith, a faith that is never daunted, a faith that never gives up and never fails. We fail to realize the largeness of our Father's supply. We forget that He has a supply that cannot be exhausted. It pleases Him when we ask for much. *"If you then, being evil, know how to give good gifts to your children, how much more will your Father who is in heaven give good things to those who ask Him!"* (Matt. 7:11). It is the *"much more"* that God shows me.

I see that God has a plan of healing. It is along the lines of perfect confidence in Him. The confidence comes not from our much speaking; it comes from our fellowship with Him. There is a wonderful fellowship with Jesus. The chief thing is to be sure that we take time for communion with Him. There is a communion with Jesus that is life and that is better than preaching.

If God definitely tells you to do anything, do it, but be sure it is God who is telling you.

The Preciousness of God's Word

I used to work with a man who had been a Baptist minister for twenty years. He was one of the sweetest souls I have ever met. He was getting to be an old man, and I used to walk by his side and listen to his instruction. God made the Word in his hand as a two-edged sword to me (see Hebrews 4:12), and I used to say, "Yes, Lord."

If the Sword ever comes to you, never harden yourself against it, but let it pierce you. You must be yielded to the Word of God. The Word will work out love in our hearts, and when practical love is in our hearts, there is no room to boast about ourselves. We see ourselves as nothing when we get lost in this divine love.

This man of God used to prune and prune me with the Sword of God, and God's Word is just as sweet to me today as it was then.

I praise God for the Sword that cuts us, and for a tender conscience. Oh, for that sweetness of fellowship with Jesus that when you hurt a fellow believer by word or act you can never let it rest until you make it right. First, we need to be converted, to become like little children (Matt. 18:3), and to have the hard heart taken away—to have a heart that is broken and melted with the love of God.

One Woman's Last Day to Live

The man of whom I have been speaking came to me and said, "The doctor says that this is the last day that my wife has to live." I said, "Oh, Brother Clark, why don't you believe God? God can raise her up if you will only believe Him." He replied, "I have looked at you when you talked and have wept and said, 'Father, if You could give me this confidence, I would be so happy.'" I said, "Could you trust God?" I felt that the Lord would heal her.

I sent word to a certain man and asked if he would come with me to a dying woman, and I believed that if two of us would go and anoint her according to James 5:14–15, she would be raised up. This man said, "Oh, why do you come to me? I could not believe, although I believe the Lord would be sure to heal her if you would go."

Then I sent word to another man and asked him to go with me. This man could pray by the hour. When he was on his knees, he could go around the world three times and come out at the same place. I told him that whatever his impression was, to be sure to go on and pray right through. We entered the house. I asked this man to pray first. He cried in his desperation and prayed that this man might be comforted after he was left with these little motherless children, and that he might be strengthened to bear his sorrow! I could hardly wait until he was finished; my whole being was moved. I thought, "What an awful thing to bring this man all this way to pray that kind of a prayer." What was the matter with him? He was looking at the dying woman instead of looking at God. You can never pray *"the prayer of faith"* (James 5:15) if you look at the person who is needing it; there is only one place to look, and that is to Jesus. The Lord wants to help us right now to learn this truth and to keep our eyes on Him.

When this man had finished, I said to Brother Clark, "Now you pray." He took up the thread where the other man had left off and went on with the same kind of prayer. He got so down beneath the burden I thought he would never rise again, and I was glad when he was through. I could not have borne it much longer. These prayers seemed to be the most out-of-place prayers that I had ever heard; the whole atmosphere was being charged with unbelief. My soul was stirred. I was eager for God to get a chance to do something and to have His way. I did not wait to pray but rushed up to the bed and tipped the oil bottle, pouring nearly the whole contents on the woman. Then I saw Jesus just above the bed with the sweetest smile on His face, and I said to her, "Woman, Jesus Christ makes you whole." The woman stood up, perfectly healed, and she is a strong woman today.

Oh, beloved, may God help us to get our eyes off the conditions and symptoms, no matter how bad they may be, and get them fastened on Him. Then we will be able to pray *"the prayer of faith"* (James 5:15).

Four

Deliverance to the Captives

ur precious Lord Jesus has everything for everybody. Forgiveness of sin, healing of diseases, and the fullness of the Spirit all come from one source—from the Lord Jesus Christ. Hear Him who is *"the same yesterday, today, and forever"* (Heb. 13:8) as He announces the purpose for which He came:

> *The Spirit of the LORD is upon Me, because He has anointed Me to preach the gospel to the poor; He has sent Me to heal the broken-hearted, to proclaim liberty to the captives and recovery of sight to the blind, to set at liberty those who are oppressed; to proclaim the acceptable year of the LORD.*   *(Luke 4:18–19)*

God's Power Is Available to You

Jesus was baptized by John in the Jordan, and the Holy Spirit descended in a bodily shape like a dove upon Him. Being full of the Holy Spirit, He was led by the Spirit into the wilderness, there to emerge more than a conqueror over the Archenemy. Then He returned *"in the power of the Spirit to Galilee"* (Luke 4:13) and preached in the synagogues. At last He came to His old hometown, Nazareth, where He announced His mission in the words I have just quoted from Luke 4:18–19. For a brief while, He ministered on the earth, and then He gave His life a ransom for all. But God raised Him from the dead.

Before Jesus went to heaven, He told His disciples that they would receive the power of the Holy Spirit upon them, too (Acts 1:8). Thus, through them, His gracious ministry would continue. This power of the Holy Spirit was not only for a few apostles, but even for those who were afar off, even as many as our God would call (Acts 2:39), even for us way down in this century. Some ask, "But wasn't this power just for the privileged few in the first century?" No. Read the Master's Great Commission as recorded in Mark 16:15–18, and you will see it is for those who believe.

The Purpose of the Power

After I received the baptism in the Holy Spirit—and I know that I received it, for the Lord gave me the Spirit in just the same way that He gave Him to the disciples at Jerusalem—I sought the mind of the Lord as to why I had been baptized. One day I came home from work and went into the house, and my wife asked me, "Which way did you come in?" I told her that I had come in the back door. She said, "There is a woman upstairs, and she has brought an eighty-year-old man to be prayed for. He is raving up there, and a great crowd has gathered outside the front door, ringing the doorbell and wanting to know what is going on in the house." The Lord quietly whispered, "This is what I baptized you for."

I carefully opened the door of the room where the man was, desiring to be obedient to what my Lord would say to me. The man was crying and shouting in distress, "I am lost! I am lost! I have committed the unpardonable sin. I am lost! I am lost!" My wife asked, "Smith, what should we do?" The Spirit of the Lord moved me to cry out, "Come out, you lying spirit." In a moment the evil spirit went, and the man was free. God gives deliverance to the captives! And the Lord said again to me, "This is what I baptized you for."

There is a place where God, through the power of the Holy Spirit, reigns supreme in our lives. The Spirit reveals, unfolds, takes of the things of Christ and shows them to us (John 16:15), and prepares us to be more than a match for satanic forces.

Miracles Are for Today

When Nicodemus came to Jesus, he said, *"Rabbi, we know that You are a teacher come from God; for no one can do these signs that You do unless God is with him"* (John 3:2). Jesus replied, *"Most assuredly, I say to you, unless one is born again, he cannot see the kingdom of God"* (v. 3).

Nicodemus was struck by Jesus' miracles, and Jesus pointed out the necessity of a miracle being done in every man who would see the kingdom. When a man is born of God—is brought from darkness to light—a mighty miracle is performed. Jesus saw every touch of God as a miracle, and so we may expect to see miracles today. It is wonderful to have the Spirit of the Lord upon us. I would rather have the Spirit of God on me for five minutes than receive a million dollars.

The Antidote for Unbelief

Do you see how Jesus mastered the Devil in the wilderness? (See Luke 4:1–14.) Jesus knew He was the Son of God, and Satan came along with an "if." How many times has Satan come along to you this way? He says, "After all, you may be deceived. You know you really are not a child of God." If the Devil comes along and says that you are not saved, it is a pretty sure sign that you are. When he comes and tells you that you are not healed, it may be taken as good evidence that the Lord has sent His Word and healed you (Ps. 107:20). The Devil knows that if he can capture your thought life, he has won a mighty victory over you. His great business is injecting thoughts, but if you are pure and holy, you will instantly shrink from them. God wants us to let the mind that was in Christ Jesus, that pure, holy, humble mind of Christ, be in us (Phil. 2:5).

I come across people everywhere I go who are held bound by deceptive conditions, and these conditions have come about simply because they have allowed the Devil to make their minds the place of his stronghold. How are we to guard against this? The Lord has provided us with weapons that are mighty through God for the pulling down of these strongholds of the Enemy (2 Cor. 10:4), by means of which every thought will be brought *"into captivity to the obedience of Christ"* (v. 5). Jesus' blood and His mighty name are an antidote to all the subtle seeds of unbelief that Satan would sow in your mind.

Christ's Amazing Works Today

In the first chapter of Acts, we see that Jesus commanded the disciples to *"wait for the Promise of the Father"* (v. 4). He told them that not many days from then they would be baptized in the Holy Spirit (v. 5). Luke told us that he had written his former account concerning *"all that Jesus began both to do and teach"* (v. 1). The ministry of Christ did not end at the Cross, but the book of Acts and the Epistles give us accounts of what He continued to do and teach through those whom He indwelt. And our blessed Lord Jesus is still alive and still continues His ministry through those who are filled with His Spirit. He is still healing the brokenhearted and delivering the captives through those on whom He places His Spirit.

I was traveling one day on a train in Sweden. At one station, an old lady boarded with her daughter. That old lady's expression was so troubled that I asked what was the matter with her. I heard that she was going to the hospital to have her leg amputated. She began to weep as she told me that the doctors had said that there was no hope for her except through having her leg amputated. She was seventy years old. I said to my interpreter, "Tell her that Jesus can heal her." The instant this was said to her, it was as though a veil had been taken off her face, it became so radiant. We stopped at another station, and the train filled up with people. A large group of men rushed to board the train, and the

Devil said, "You're done." But I knew I had the best situation, for hard things are always opportunities to gain more glory for the Lord as He manifests His power.

Every trial is a blessing. There have been times when I have been hard-pressed through circumstances, and it seemed as if a dozen steamrollers were going over me, but I have found that the hardest things are just lifting places into the grace of God. We have such a lovely Jesus. He always proves Himself to be such a mighty Deliverer. He never fails to plan the best things for us.

The train began moving, and I crouched down and in the name of Jesus commanded the disease to leave. The old lady cried, "I'm healed! I know I'm healed!" She stamped her leg and said, "I'm going to prove it." So when we stopped at another station, she marched up and down and shouted, "I'm not going to the hospital." Once again our wonderful Jesus had proven Himself a Healer of the brokenhearted, a Deliverer of one who was bound.

My Own Remarkable Healing

At one time I was so bound that no human power could help me. My wife thought that I would pass away. There was no help. At that time I had just had a faint glimpse of Jesus as the Healer. For six months I had been suffering from appendicitis, occasionally getting temporary relief. I went to the mission of which I was the pastor, but I was brought to the floor in awful agony, and I was brought home to my bed. All night I was praying, pleading for deliverance, but none came. My wife was sure it was my call home to heaven and sent for a physician. He said that there was no possible chance for me—my body was too weak. Having had the appendicitis for six months, my whole system was drained, and, because of that, he thought that it was too late for an operation. He left my wife in a state of brokenheartedness.

After he left, a young man and an old lady came to our door. I knew that the old lady was a woman of real prayer. They came upstairs to my room. This young man jumped on the bed and commanded the evil spirit to come out of me. He shouted, "Come out, you devil! I command you to come out in the name of Jesus!" There was no chance for an argument or for me to tell him that I would never believe that there was a devil inside of me. The thing had to go in the name of Jesus, and it went. I was instantly healed.

I arose and dressed and went downstairs. I was still in the plumbing business, and I asked my wife, "Is there any work in? I'm all right now, and I am going to work." I found that there was a certain job to be done, and I picked up my tools and went off to do it. Just after I left, the doctor came in, put his hat down in the hall, and walked up to the bedroom. But the invalid was not there. "Where is Mr. Wigglesworth?" he asked. "Oh, doctor, he's gone out to work," said my wife. "You'll never see him alive again," said the doctor; "they'll bring him back a corpse."

Well, you see before you the corpse.

Since that time the Lord has given me the privilege of praying for people with appendicitis in many parts of the world, and I have seen a great many people up and dressed within a quarter of an hour from the time I prayed for them. We have a living Christ who is willing to meet people in every place.

A Man Whose Bride Was Dying

About eight years ago I met Brother Kerr, and he gave me a letter of introduction to a brother in Zion City named Cook. I took his letter to Brother Cook, and he said, "God has sent you here." He gave me the addresses of six people and asked me to go and pray for them and meet him again at twelve o'clock. I got back at about 12:30, and he told me about a young man who was to be married the following Monday. His sweetheart was dying of appendicitis. I went to the house and found that the physician had just been there and had pronounced that there was no hope. The mother was distraught and was pulling her hair and saying, "Is there no deliverance?" I said to her, "Woman, believe God, and your daughter will be healed and be up and dressed in fifteen minutes." But the mother went on screaming.

They took me into the bedroom, and I prayed for the girl and commanded the evil spirit to depart in the name of Jesus. She cried, "I am healed." I said to her, "Do you want me to believe that you are healed? If you are healed, get up." She said, "You get out of the room, and I'll get up." In less than ten minutes the doctor came in. He wanted to know what had happened. She said, "A man came in and prayed for me, and I am healed." The doctor pressed his finger right in the place that had been so sore, and the girl neither moaned nor cried. He said, "This is God." It made no difference whether he acknowledged it or not; I knew that God had worked.

Our God is real, and He has saving and healing power today. Our Jesus is just the same *"yesterday, today, and forever"* (Heb. 13:8). He saves and heals today just as of old, and He wants to be your Savior and your Healer.

Oh, if you would only believe God! What would happen? The greatest things. Some have never tasted the grace of God, have never had the peace of God. Unbelief robs them of these blessings. It is possible to hear and yet not perceive the truth. It is possible to read the Word and not share in the life it brings. It is necessary for us to have the Holy Spirit to unfold the Word and bring to us the life that is Christ. We can never fully understand the wonders of this redemption until we are full of the Holy Spirit.

Disease due to Immorality

One time I was at an afternoon meeting. The Lord had been graciously with us, and many had been healed by the power of God. Most of the people had gone home when I saw a young man who evidently was hanging back to have a word with me. I asked, "What do you want?" He said, "I wonder if I could ask you to pray for me." I said, "What's the trouble?" He said, "Can't you smell?" The young man had gone into sin and was suffering the consequences. He said, "I have been turned out of two hospitals. I am broken out all over. I have abscesses all over me." I could see that he was badly broken out on his nose. He said, "I heard you preach and could not understand about this healing business, and I was wondering if there was any hope for me."

I asked him, "Do you know Jesus?" He did not know the first thing about salvation, but I said to him, "Stand still." I placed my hands on him and cursed that terrible disease in the name of Jesus. He cried out, "I know I'm healed. I can feel a warmth and a glow all over me." I said, "Who did it?" He said, "Your prayers." I said, "No, it was Jesus!" He said, "Was it He? Oh, Jesus! Jesus! Jesus, save me." And that young man went away healed and saved. Oh, what a merciful God we have! What a wonderful Jesus is ours!

A Place of Deliverance

Are you oppressed? Cry out to God. It is always good for people to cry out. You may have to cry out. The Holy Spirit and the Word of God will bring to light every hidden, unclean thing that must be revealed. There is always a place of deliverance when you let God search out what is spoiling and marring your life.

That evil spirit that was in the man in the synagogue cried out, *"Let us alone!"* (Mark 1:24). It is notable that that evil spirit never cried out like that until Jesus walked into the place where he was. Jesus rebuked the thing, saying, *"Be quiet, and come out of him!"* (v. 25), and the man was delivered. He is just the same Jesus, exposing the powers of evil, delivering the captives and letting the oppressed go free, purifying them and cleansing their hearts.

The evil spirits that inhabited the man who had the legion did not want to be sent to the pit to be tormented before their time, and so they cried out to be sent into the swine. (See Luke 8:27–35.) Hell is such an awful place that even the demons hate the thought of going there. How much more should men seek to be saved from the pit?

God is compassionate and says, *"Seek the LORD while He may be found"* (Isa. 55:6). He has further stated, *"Whoever calls on the name of the LORD shall be saved"* (Acts 2:21). Seek Him now; call on His name right now. There is forgiveness, healing, redemption, deliverance—everything you need right here and now, and that which will satisfy you throughout eternity.

Five

Dare To Believe God!
Then Command!

Most assuredly, I say to you, he who believes in Me,
the works that I do he will do also; and greater works
than these he will do, because I go to My Father. And
whatever you ask in My name, that I will do, that the
Father may be glorified in the Son. If you ask
anything in My name, I will do it.
—John 14:12–14

 e who believes." What a word! God's Word changes us, and we enter into fellowship and communion. We enter into assurance and Godlikeness, for we see the truth and believe. Faith is an effective power; God opens the understanding and reveals Himself. *"Therefore it is of faith that it might be according to grace"* (Rom. 4:16). Grace is God's blessing coming down to you. You open the door to God as an act of faith, and God does all you want.

Jesus drew the hearts of the people to Himself. They came to Him with all of their needs, and He relieved them all. He talked to men, healed the sick, relieved the oppressed, and cast out demons. *"He who believes in Me, the works that I do he will do also"* (John 14:12).

"He who believes in Me"—the essence of divine life is in us by faith. To the one who believes, it will come to pass. We become supernatural by the power of God. If you believe, the power of the Enemy cannot stand, for God's Word is against him. Jesus gives us His Word to make faith effective. If you can believe in your heart, you begin to speak whatever you desire, and whatever you dare to say is done. You will have whatever you say after you believe in your heart. (See Mark 11:23–24.) Dare to believe, and then dare to speak, for you will have whatever you say if you do not doubt.

Some time ago in England, the power of God was on the meeting, and I was telling the people they could be healed. I said that if they would rise up, I would pray for them, and the Lord would heal them. A man with broken ribs was healed. Then a fourteen-year-old girl said, "Will you pray for me?" After I prayed for her, she said, "Mother, I am being healed." She had straps on her feet, and when these were removed, God healed her right away. Dare to believe God, and it will be as you believe.

Six

The Power to Bind and to Loose

Then the Pharisees and Sadducees came,
and testing Him asked that He would show them a
sign from heaven. He answered and said to them,
"When it is evening you say, 'It will be fair weather,
for the sky is red'; and in the morning, 'It will be foul
weather today, for the sky is red and threatening.'
Hypocrites! You know how to discern the face of the
sky, but you cannot discern the signs of the times. A
wicked and adulterous generation seeks after
a sign, and no sign shall be given to it except
the sign of the prophet Jonah."
—Matthew 16:1–4

he Pharisees and Sadducees had been tempting Jesus to show them a sign from heaven. He told them that they could discern the signs that appeared on the face of the sky and yet could not discern the signs of the times. He would give them no sign to satisfy their unbelieving curiosity, remarking that a wicked and adulterous generation sought a sign and that no sign would be given to them except the sign of the prophet Jonah. A wicked and adulterous generation stumbles over the story of Jonah, but faith can see in that story a wonderful picture of the death, burial, and resurrection of our Lord Jesus Christ.

Remember God's Goodness

After Jesus had departed from the Pharisees, He said to His disciples, *"Take heed and beware of the leaven of the Pharisees and the Sadducees"* (Matt. 16:6). The disciples began to discuss this among themselves, and all they could think of was that they had brought no bread. What were they going to do? Then Jesus uttered these words: *"O you of little faith"* (v. 8). He had been with them for quite a while, yet they were still a great disappointment to Him because of their lack of comprehension and of faith. They could not grasp the profound spiritual truth He was bringing to them and could only think about having brought no bread. So Jesus said to them,

> *O you of little faith...Do you not yet under-*
> *stand, or remember the five loaves of the five*
> *thousand and how many baskets you took up?*
> *Nor the seven loaves of the four thousand and*
> *how many large baskets you took up?*
> *(Matt. 16:8–10)*

Do you keep in mind how God has been gracious in the past? God has done wonderful things for all of us. If we keep these things in mind, we will become *"strong in faith"* (Rom. 4:20 KJV). We should be able to defy Satan in everything. Remember that the Lord has led all the way. When Joshua passed over the Jordan on dry land, he told the people to pick up twelve stones and set them up in Gilgal. These were to be a constant reminder to the children of Israel that they came over the Jordan on dry land. (See Joshua 4:20–24.) How many times had Jesus shown to His disciples the mightiness of His power? Yet they failed in faith right here.

The Power in Jesus' Words

One time Jesus had the following conversation with Peter:

> *"What do you think, Simon? From whom do the kings of the earth take customs or taxes, from their sons or from strangers?" Peter said to Him, "From strangers." Jesus said to him, "Then the sons are free. Nevertheless, lest we offend them, go to the sea, cast in a hook, and take the fish that comes up first. And when you have opened its mouth, you will find a piece of money; take that and give it to them for Me and you."* (Matt. 17:25–27)

Peter had been in the fishing business all his life, but he had never caught a fish with silver in its mouth. However, the Master does not want us to reason things out, for carnal reasoning will always land us in a bog of unbelief. He wants us simply to obey. "This is a hard job," Peter must have said as he put the bait on his hook, "but since You told me to do it, I'll try." And he cast his line into the sea. There were millions of fish in the sea, but every fish had to stand aside and leave that bait alone and let the fish with the piece of money in its mouth come up and take it.

Do you not see that the words of the Master are the instruction of faith? It is impossible for anything that Jesus says to miss. All His words are spirit and life (John 6:63). If you will only have faith in Him, you will find that every word that God gives is life. You cannot be in close contact with Him and receive His Word in simple faith without feeling the effect of it in your body, as well as in your spirit and soul.

A woman came to me in Cardiff, Wales, who was filled with ulcers. She had fallen in the streets twice because of this trouble. When she came to the meeting, it seemed as if the evil power within her purposed to kill her right there. She fell, and the power of the Devil was attacking her severely. Not only was she helpless, but it seemed as if she had died. I cried, "O God, help this woman." Then I rebuked the evil power in the name of Jesus, and instantly the Lord healed her. She rose up and made a great to-do. She felt the power of God in her body and wanted to testify continually. After three days she went to another place and began to testify about the Lord's power to heal. She came to me and said, "I want to tell everyone about the Lord's healing power. Don't you have any tracts on this subject?" I handed her my Bible and said, "Matthew, Mark, Luke, and John—they are the best tracts on healing. They are full of incidents of the healing power of Jesus. They will never fail to accomplish the work of God if people will only read and believe them."

That is where men are lacking. All lack of faith is due to not feeding on God's Word. You need it every day. How can you enter into a life of faith? Feed on the living Christ of whom this Word is full. As you are taken up with the glorious fact and the wondrous presence of the living Christ, the faith of God will spring up within you. *"Faith comes by hearing, and hearing by the word of God"* (Rom. 10:17).

A Personal Revelation from God

Jesus asked His disciples who men were saying that He was. They told Him, *"Some say John the Baptist, some Elijah, and others Jeremiah or one of the prophets"* (Matt. 16:14). Then He put the question to His disciples to see what they thought: *"But who do you say that I am?"* (v. 15). Peter answered, *"You are the Christ, the Son of the living God"* (v. 16). And Jesus said to him, *"Blessed are you, Simon Bar-Jonah, for flesh and blood has not revealed this to you, but My Father who is in heaven"* (v. 17).

It is so simple. Who do you say He is? Who is He? Do you say with Peter, *"You are the Christ, the Son of the living God"*? How can you know this? He must be revealed to you. Flesh and blood do not reveal His identity; it is an inward revelation. God wants to reveal His Son within us and make us conscious of an inward presence. Then you can cry out, "I know He's mine. He's mine! He's mine!" *"Nor does anyone know the Father except the Son, and the one to whom the Son wills to **reveal** Him"* (Matt. 11:27, emphasis added). Seek God until you get from Him a mighty revelation of the Son, until that inward revelation moves you on to the place where you are always *"steadfast, immovable, always abounding in the work of the Lord"* (1 Cor. 15:58).

There is a wonderful power in this revelation. When Peter said to Jesus, *"You are the Christ"* (Matt. 16:16), He replied,

> *On this rock I will build My church, and the gates of Hades shall not prevail against it. And I will give you the keys of the kingdom of heaven, and whatever you bind on earth will be bound in heaven, and whatever you loose on earth will be loosed in heaven. (Matt. 16:18–19)*

Was Peter the rock? No. A few minutes later he was so full of the Devil that Christ had to say to him, *"Get behind Me, Satan! You are an offense to Me"* (v. 23). This rock was Christ. He is the Rock; there are many Scriptures to confirm this. And to everyone who knows that He is the Christ, He gives the key of faith, the power to bind and the power to loose. Establish your hearts with this fact. God wants you to have the inward revelation of this truth and of all the power contained in it.

Wonderful Demonstrations of God's Might

"On this rock I will build My church, and the gates of Hades shall not prevail against it" (v. 18). God is pleased when we stand on the Rock and believe that He is unchangeable. If you will dare to believe God, you can defy all the powers of evil. There have been times in my experience when I have dared to believe Him and have had the most remarkable experiences.

One day I was traveling in a railway coach, and there were two people in the coach who were very sick, a mother and her daughter. I said to them, "Look, I've something in this bag that will cure every case in the world. It has never been known to fail." They became very much interested, and I went on to tell them more and more about this remedy that had never failed to remove disease and sickness. At last they summoned up the courage to ask for a dose. So I opened my bag, took out my Bible, and read them the verse that says, *"I am the LORD who heals you"* (Exod. 15:26).

God's Word never fails. He will always heal you if you dare to believe Him. Men are searching everywhere today for things with which they can heal themselves, and they ignore the fact that the Balm of Gilead is within easy reach. As I talked about this wonderful Physician, the faith of both mother and daughter went out toward Him, and He healed them both right in the train.

God has made His Word so precious that if I could not get another copy of it, I would not part with my Bible for all the world. There is life in the Word. There is power in it. I find Christ in it, and He is the One I need for spirit, soul, and body. It tells me of the power of His name and the power of His blood for cleansing. *"The young lions lack and suffer hunger; but those who seek the LORD shall not lack any good thing"* (Ps. 34:10).

A man came to me one time, brought by a little woman. I said, "What seems to be the problem?" She said, "He gets employment, but he fails every time. He is a slave to alcohol and nicotine poison. He is a bright, intelligent man in most areas, but he is in bondage to these two things." I was reminded of the words of the Master, giving us power to bind and to loose, and I told him to stick out his tongue. In the name of the Lord Jesus Christ, I cast out the evil powers that gave him the taste for these things. I said to him, "Man, you are free today." He was unsaved, but when he realized the power of the Lord in delivering him, he came to the services, publicly acknowledged that he was sinner, and was saved and baptized. A few days later I asked, "How are things with you?" He said, "I'm delivered." God has given us the power to bind and the power to loose.

Another person came and said, "What can you do for me? I have had sixteen operations and have had my eardrums taken out." I said, "God has not forgotten how to make eardrums." She was so deaf that I do not think she would have heard a cannon go off. I anointed her and prayed, asking the Lord to replace the eardrums. But she remained as deaf as it was possible to be afterward. However, she saw other people getting healed and rejoicing. Had *"God forgotten to be gracious"* (Ps. 77:9)? Wasn't His power just the same? She came the next night and said, "I have come to believe God tonight." Take care you do not come any other way. I prayed for her again and commanded her ears to be loosed in the name of Jesus. She believed, and the moment she believed, she heard. She ran and jumped on a chair and began to preach. Later I let a pin drop, and she heard it touch the floor. God can give drums to ears. *"With God all things are possible"* (Matt. 19:26). God can save the worst case.

Discouraged one, *"cast your burden on the LORD, and He shall sustain you"* (Ps. 55:22). Look to Him and be radiant (Ps. 34:5). Look to Him now.

Seven

You Are the Christ

 need not say how pleased I am to be among you again. We are coming in contact this afternoon with a living Christ. It is on the Rock that God is building His church, and the gates of hell will not prevail against it (Matt. 16:18).

We are more confident today than we were yesterday. God is building us up in this faith, so that we are living in great expectation. He is bringing us into a place with Himself where we can say, "I have seen God."

I have been asking God to send us something on fire from His Word—something that will live in our hearts, that will abide with us forever. It is important that every day we lay some new foundation that can never be uprooted. Oh, for a living touch from God, a new inspiration of power, and a deeper sense of His love!

The Key to All Real Success

I have been thinking about the sixteenth chapter of Matthew and Peter's answer to Jesus when He asked His disciples the question, *"Who do you say that I am?"* (Matt. 16:15). Peter answered, *"You are the Christ, the Son of the living God"* (v. 16). Beloved friend, do you know Him? Has this revelation come to your heart? Do you call Him Lord? Do you find comfort in the fact that He is yours?

"Who do you say that I am?" The Master knew what was in their thoughts before He asked them. This fact makes me long more and more to be really true; God is seeing right into my heart and reads my thoughts.

There is something in what Jesus said to Peter that is applicable to us: *"Blessed are you, Simon Bar-Jonah, for flesh and blood has not revealed this to you, but My Father who is in heaven"* (v. 17). If you can call Jesus Lord, it is by the Holy Spirit (1 Cor. 12:3). Therefore, there ought to be within us a deep response that says, *"You are the Christ"* (Matt. 16:16). When we can say this from our hearts, we know that we are not born of flesh and blood, but of the Spirit of the living God. (See John 3:5–6.)

If you will go back to the time when you first had the knowledge that you were born of God, you will see that there was within you a deep cry for your Father. You found you have a heavenly Father. If you want to know the real success of any life, it is because of this knowledge: *"You are the Christ."* This knowledge is the rock foundation, and the gates of hell will not prevail against it (Matt. 16:18). *"And I will give you the keys of the kingdom of heaven"* (v. 19).

It is about this rock, this blessed foundation truth, that I want to speak this afternoon—this knowledge of our personal acceptance by God, this life of faith that we have come into. It is because of this rock foundation that we have this living faith, and this foundation cannot be overthrown. Jesus has given us power to bind and to loose (Matt. 16:19). Everyone who has come to this rock foundation ought to be in this position. I want you to go away from this meeting knowing that you are on this rock foundation and are able to bind and able to loose, having that living faith so that you can pray and *know* you have the answer because of God's promises. It is on this rock that our faith must be based, and it will never fail; God has established it forever.

How to Obtain Spiritual Power

From that time Jesus began to show to His disciples that He must go to Jerusalem, and suffer many things from the elders and chief priests and scribes, and be killed, and be raised the third day. Then Peter took Him aside and began to rebuke Him, saying, "Far be it from You, Lord; this shall not happen to You!" But He turned and said to Peter, "Get behind Me, Satan! You are an offense to Me, for you are not mindful of the things of God, but the things of men." Then Jesus said to His disciples, "If anyone desires to come after Me, let him deny himself, and take up his cross, and follow Me."   *(Matt. 16:21–24)*

We find that the fundamental truths of all the ages were planted right in the life of Peter. We see evidences of the spiritual power to which he had attained, and we see also the natural power working.

Jesus saw that He must suffer if He would reach the spiritual life that God intended Him to reach. So Jesus said, "I must go forward. Your words, Peter, are an offense to Me." If you to seek to save yourself, it is an offense to God. God has been impressing on me more and more that if at any time I were to seek man's favor or earthly power, I would lose favor with God and could not have faith. Jesus asked, *"How can you believe* [if you] *receive honor from one another?"* (John 5:44).

God is speaking to us, every one of us, and trying to get us to leave the shoreline. There is only one place where we can get the mind and will of God; it is alone with God. If we look to anybody else, we cannot get it. If we seek to save ourselves, we will never reach the place where we will be able to bind and loose. There is a close companionship between you and Jesus that nobody knows about, where every day you have to choose or refuse.

It is in the narrow way that you get the power to bind and the power to loose. I know that Jesus was separated from His own family and friends. He was deprived of the luxuries of life. It seems to me that God wants to get every one of us separated to Himself in this holy war, and we are not going to have faith if we do not give ourselves wholly to Him. Beloved, it is in these last days that I cannot have the power I want to have unless, as a sheep, I am willing to shear myself. The way is narrow. (See Matthew 7:13–14.)

Beloved, you will not be able to bind and loose if you have sin in you. There is not one person who is able to deal with the sins of others if he is not free himself. *"He breathed on them, and said to them,*

'Receive the Holy Spirit'" (John 20:22). He knew the
Holy Spirit would give them both a revelation of
themselves and a revelation of God. He must reveal
to you your depravity. In Luke 22:29–30, we read,

> *And I bestow upon you a kingdom, just as My
> Father bestowed one upon Me, that you may
> eat and drink at My table in My kingdom, and
> sit on thrones judging the twelve tribes of Is-
> rael.*

Do you believe that the Father in heaven would
make you a judge over a kingdom if there were anything crooked in you? Do you believe you will be able
to bind unless you are free yourself? But everyone
who has this living Christ within him has the power
that will put to death all sin.

With Jesus' last words on earth, He gave the
disciples a commission. (See Mark 16:15–18.) The
discipleship has never ceased. The churches are
weak today because Christ the Rock is not abiding in
them in the manifestations of the power of God. This
is not because it is a special gift—this power to bind
and loose—but it is contingent on whether you have
the rock foundation in you. In the name of Jesus,
you will loose, and in the name of Jesus, you will
bind. If He is in you, you ought to bring forth evidences of that power.

One can see that Peter had great sympathy in
the natural, and he did not want Jesus to be crucified. It was perfectly natural for Peter to say what
he did, but Jesus said, *"Get behind Me"* (Matt.
16:23). He knew He must not be turned aside by any
human sympathy. The only way we can retain our

humility is to stay on this narrow line and say, "Get behind me, Satan." If you try to go the easy way, you cannot be Jesus' disciple (Luke 14:27).

Beloved, we are now living in the experience of the fact that Jesus is the Rock. I am glad, for we are within reach of wonderful possibilities because of the Rock. Take a stand on the fact that the Rock cannot be overthrown.

Many Examples of God's Healing Touch

At one meeting, there was a seventy-seven-year-old woman who was paralyzed. The power of God came into her, and she was so strengthened and blessed after prayer that she rushed up and down in a marvelous way.

Brothers and sisters, what I see in this woman's healing is an illustration of what God will do. I am trusting that we will all be so strengthened today with the power of God that we will not allow any doubt or fear to come into our hearts. On the contrary, we will know that we are created anew by a living faith and that there is in that faith within us power to accomplish wonderful things for God.

I want to say that the most wonderful and marvelous faith is the simple faith of a little child. It is the faith that dares. There is a boldness in childlike faith that causes us to say, "You will be healed."

A man brought his son to my meeting, and he was all drawn to one side from having fits for years. The father asked, "Can you do anything for my son?" I said in the name of Jesus, "Yes, he can be healed." I knew it was because of the Rock that it could be done. There is a Spirit who dwells within us, and He is nothing less than the life of Him who gave Himself for us, for He is the life of the Rock in us.

I wonder if you wait until some mighty power sweeps over you before you feel you have power to bind. That is not the power. The Rock is within you; you have power to bind and power to loose because you consist of the Rock. What you have to do is stand on that fact and use the power. Will you do it?

I said, "Father, in the name of Jesus, I bind the evil spirit in this young man." Oh, the name of Jesus! We make too little use of that name. Even the children cried, *"Hosanna"* (Matt. 21:15). If we would let ourselves go and praise Him more and more, God would give us the shout of victory.

The father brought the young man to the next meeting, and I did not need to ask if he was delivered. The brightness of his face and the shining of the father's face told the story. But I asked, "Is he all right now?" and he said, "Yes."

Oh, I see it is needed so much, this power to bind and power to loose. Brothers and sisters, wherever you are, you can set people free. God wants to change your name from Doubting Thomas to Prevailing Israel.

A young woman was brought to me who had cancer. Her spirits were very low. People need to be made glad. I said to her, "Cheer up," but I could not get her to cheer up. So I bound the evil power in the name of Jesus and then laid my hands on her and said, "Sister, you are free." She arose and asked if she could say something. She rubbed the place where the cancer had been and said, "It is all gone!"

Oh, brothers and sisters, I want you to see that that power is yours. God is delighted when we use the power He has given us. I believe every child of God has a measure of this power, but there is a fuller manifestation of the power when we get so filled that we speak in tongues. I want you to press on until you get the fullness. I must send you home with a loaf of bread and a cake of raisins, as David did with the people. (See 2 Samuel 6:19.)

When will we see all the people filled with the Holy Spirit and things done as they were in the Acts of the Apostles? It will be when all the people say, "Lord, You are God." I want you to come into a place of such relationship with God that you will know your prayers are answered because He has promised.

I dropped into a shoemaker's shop one morning, and there was a man who had his eyes covered with a green shade. They were so inflamed that he was suffering terribly. He said, "I cannot rest anywhere." I did not ask him what he believed but laid down my Bible and put my hands on those poor suffering eyes in the name of Jesus. He said, "This is strange; I have no pain. I am free."

Do you think the human mind can do that? I say, "No." We do these things with a consciousness that God will answer, and He is pleased with that kind of service.

A boy came into a meeting on crutches. He had a broken ankle. Several of us joined in prayer, and with joy I saw the boy so healed that he walked away carrying his crutches.

Beloved, Jesus is coming soon. There are so many things that seem to say, "He is at the door." Will you use the power of the Rock within you for His glory?

Eight

How Multitudes
Were Delivered

acts are stubborn things. We want all unbelief cut away so that the mind does not
interfere with God's plan. The Devil has
been at work. Men today try to put away
what God has established. God has established truth
in His Word, but men have tried to bring it to nothing. God has His Word in the earth; it is also *"settled
in heaven"* (Ps. 119:89). If you are standing on the
Word, you are eternally fixed. God has said it, and it
is established; the Word of God *"abides forever"* (1
Pet. 1:23). Men pass away, things change, but God's
Word *"abides forever."* Examine yourselves in the
faith (2 Cor. 13:5).

Someone Greater than Satan

"If You are willing, You can make me clean"
(Matt. 8:2). Who said this? A leper. In Bible times,
leprosy was incurable. It is a loathsome condition in
which limbs rot and fall off. When a man had leprosy,

he was doomed for life. Like cancer or tuberculosis, it was the Devil manifest in the flesh. And the Devil never lets go of the flesh until he is forced to. For deliverance you must have someone mightier than Satan. Here is a fact: in our midst is One greater than Satan. If you believe it, it will make all the difference to you. It will mean no more trouble, no more sickness. God's plan is wonderful. Allow God to do a deep work, cutting away unbelief. His ways are perfect.

Jesus always goes to the right place. Sometimes doctors say that they begin to operate at the wrong place and that when they get to the right place, they cannot do what is needed. When the patient dies, they say the operation was successful but that he died after it. No one dies after the operation of Jesus. This is rather hard on the doctors, some say. No, they need not worry; they will have plenty to do while the world is rolling on in sin. But the believer is in a place quite different from that of the world. Jesus asked the woman, "Can we take the children's bread and give it to the dogs?" (See Matthew 15:26.) Children of God have bread; it is the life of Jesus. Jesus has all the bread you want, for spirit, soul, and body.

I went into a hotel where there was a man whose arm had been poisoned. I looked at the arm; it was very swollen. His arm, neck, and face were blue. He opened his eyes and said, "Can you save me? I am dying." I took hold of the arm and turned it round twice. It was an act of faith. I said, "In the name of Jesus, you are free." He swung his arm round and round and said, "Look! Jesus is that mighty, wonderful name, which God has said is greater than all." This same Jesus is the Deliverer of all humanity.

You Can Be Free

Women often say to their children, "Run and fetch my purse; I cannot get along without my purse." Mother, have you ever run back for your Bible? It contains richer gold and greater power. If the Word of God is in your heart, you will be free. God is always making you free. The Gospel is full of liberty and has no bondage. It is full of liberty! How long does it take to get clean? Jesus said to the leper, *"I am willing; be cleansed"* (Matt. 8:3), and his leprosy was cleansed immediately.

Lots of people have a big barrier in their way. They say, "I wonder if it is God's will," and they hang their harps on the willows. (See Psalm 137:1–4.) Is it the will of God? The answer comes when we look at redemption. Is it the will of God to save? Some people say, "All men will be saved." That is not scriptural. Who will be saved, and who will be lost? The lost are those who do not believe. To all who believe, God's plan is clear. The plan is "I will when you will."

The Power of True Faith

There was a woman sick and near death. She sent for me. I went with a mission leader to her house. There she was, lying in bed, dying. The Lord revealed to me that nothing could save her except His power. I bent near to her. She said, "I have faith; I have faith." She repeated this continually: "I have faith." I said, "You have no faith; you are dying, and you know it. You have only words." I asked her, "Do you want to live?" "Yes," she said, "but I have no power." The Spirit of the Lord came upon me, and I said, "In the name of Jesus." Then the Spirit of God raised her up.

Faith is actively refusing the power of the Devil. It is not saying mere words. You must have an activity of faith, refusing the conditions in the name of Jesus. We must have something more than words. Satan comes *"to kill, and to destroy"* (John 10:10). Jesus comes to give life abundantly (v. 10). He comes to give abounding life through the operation of the Holy Spirit. The leper said, *"If You are willing, You can make me clean"* (Matt. 8:2). Jesus said, *"I am willing"* (v. 3).

A Testimony of Healing

In one place where I was, there came a woman to be healed. Crowds were present. Here was a case God wanted to make an exhibition of. Here she was, in pain, in weakness, with flesh gone, unable to eat solid food. I said to the crowds, "Look at her. Take in the details of her condition." Then in the name of Jesus, I cast out the evil spirit and laid my hands upon her. She told the people she was free. She came to the meeting that night and to the one the next day, magnifying God. I was surprised to see her; I thought she had gone to her home in the country. She said, "I cannot go until I have fully magnified the Lord." When she left, she said, "Goodbye. I am going to preach this life: *'He Himself took our infirmities and bore our sicknesses'* (Matt. 8:17)."

So many miss the way because they rely on their feelings. It is more important to have God's Word than anything else. Psalm 119:50 states, *"Your word has given me life.*" Nothing but the Word can give life, and the Word is Jesus. "*Your word I have hidden in my heart*" (Ps. 119:11). All darkness, sin, and affliction must go. The Word of God is against them. You cannot have both them and the Word of God. To believe is to be saved, to be healed, to be free. Unbelief is neither salvation, healing, nor freedom. "*If you can believe, all things are possible to him who believes*" (Mark 9:23). This truth is established forever.

Nine

Life in the Spirit

*Do we begin again to commend ourselves? Or do we
need, as some others, epistles of commendation to you
or letters of commendation from you? You are our
epistle written in our hearts, known and read by all
men; clearly you are an epistle of Christ, ministered
by us, written not with ink but by the Spirit of the
living God, not on tablets of stone but on tablets of
flesh, that is, of the heart. And we have such trust
through Christ toward God. Not that we are
sufficient of ourselves to think of anything as being
from ourselves, but our sufficiency is from God, who
also made us sufficient as ministers of the new
covenant, not of the letter but of the Spirit; for the
letter kills, but the Spirit gives life. But if the
ministry of death, written and engraved on stones,
was glorious, so that the children of Israel could not
look steadily at the face of Moses because of the glory
of his countenance, which glory was passing away
["done away" KJV], how will the ministry of the
Spirit not be more glorious? For if the ministry of
condemnation had glory, the ministry of
righteousness exceeds much more in glory. For even*

*what was made glorious had no glory in this respect,
because of the glory that excels. For if what is passing
away ["done away" KJV] was glorious, what remains
is much more glorious. Therefore, since we have such
hope, we use great boldness of speech; unlike Moses,
who put a veil over his face so that the children of
Israel could not look steadily at the end of what was
passing away. But their minds were blinded. For
until this day the same veil remains unlifted in the
reading of the Old Testament, because the veil is
taken away ["done away" KJV] in Christ. But even to
this day, when Moses is read, a veil lies on their
heart. Nevertheless when one turns to the Lord, the
veil is taken away. Now the Lord is the Spirit; and
where the Spirit of the Lord is, there is liberty. But
we all, with unveiled face, beholding as in a mirror
the glory of the Lord, are being transformed into
the same image from glory to glory, just
as by the Spirit of the Lord.
—2 Corinthians 3:1–18*

 e are told in Hebrews 6:1–2 that we are to
leave the first principles of the doctrine of
Christ and go on to perfection, not laying
again the foundation of repentance from
dead works and the doctrine of baptisms and the
other first principles. What would you think of a
builder who was continually pulling down his house
and putting in fresh foundations? Never look back if
you want the power of God in your life. You will find
out that in the measure you have allowed yourself to
look back, you have missed what God had for you.

The Holy Spirit shows us that we must never
look back to the law of sin and death from which we

have been delivered. (See Romans 8:2.) God has brought us into a new order of things, a life of love and liberty in Christ Jesus that is beyond all human comprehension. Many are brought into this new life through the power of the Spirit of God, and then, like the Galatians, who ran well at the beginning, they try to perfect themselves through legalism. (See Galatians 3:1–3; 5:7.) They turn back from a life in the Spirit to a life along natural lines. God is not pleased with this, for He has no place for the person who has lost the vision. The only thing to do is to repent. Don't try to cover up anything. If you have been tripped up in any area, confess it; then look to God to bring you to a place of stability of faith where your whole walk will be in the Spirit.

The Joy of Being God's Child

We all ought to have a clear conviction that *"salvation is of the LORD"* (Jonah 2:9). Salvation is more than a human order of things. If the Enemy can move you from a place of faith, he can get you outside of the plan of God. The moment a man falls into sin, divine life ceases to flow, and his life becomes one of helplessness. But this is not God's plan for any of His children. Read the third chapter of John's first epistle, and take your place as a child of God. Take the place of knowing that you are a child of God, and remember that as your hope is set in Christ, it should have a purifying effect on your life. The Holy Spirit says, *"Whoever has been born of God does not sin, for His seed remains in him; and he cannot sin, because he has been born of God"* (1 John 3:9). There is life and power in the seed of the Word that is implanted within. God is in that *"cannot,"* and there is more power in that Word of His than in any human objections. God's thought for every one of us is that we will reign in life by Jesus Christ (Rom. 5:17). You must come to see how wonderful you are in God and how helpless you are in yourself.

God declared Himself to be mightier than every opposing power when He cast out the powers of darkness from heaven. I want you to know that the same power that cast Satan out of heaven dwells in every person who is born of God. If you would only realize this, you would *"reign in life"* (Rom. 5:17). When you see people laid out under an evil power, when you see the powers of evil manifesting themselves, always ask them the question, "Did Jesus come in the flesh?" I have never heard an evil power answer in the affirmative. (See 1 John 4:2–3.) When you know you have an evil spirit to deal with, you have power to cast it out. Believe this fact, and act on it, for *"greater is he that is in you, than he that is in the world"* (1 John 4:4 KJV). God intends for you to overcome and has put a force within you whereby you may defeat the Devil.

Triumphing in Trials

Temptations will come to all. If you are not worth tempting, you are not worth much. Job said, *"When He has tested me, I shall come forth as gold"* (Job 23:10). In every temptation that comes, the Lord allows you to be tempted to the very hilt, but He will never allow you to be defeated if you walk in obedience. Right in the midst of the temptation, He will always *"make the way of escape"* (1 Cor. 10:13).

> *An Interpretation of Tongues:* "God comes forth and with His power sweeps away the refuge of lies and all the powers of darkness and causes you always to triumph in Christ Jesus. The Lord loves His saints and covers them with His almighty wings."

May God help us to see this truth. We cannot be *"to the praise of His glory"* (Eph. 1:12) until we are ready for trials and are able to triumph in them. We cannot get away from the fact that sin came in by nature, but God comes into our nature and puts sin into the place of death. Why? So that the Spirit of God may come into the temple in all His power and liberty, and so that right here in this present, evil world Satan may be dethroned by the believer.

The Spirit's Work in Our Hearts

Satan is always endeavoring to bring the saints of God into disrepute by bringing against them slanderous accusations, but the Holy Spirit never comes with condemnation. He always reveals the blood of Christ. He always brings us help. The Lord Jesus referred to Him as the Comforter who would come (John 14:16 KJV). He is always on hand to help in the seasons of testing and trial. The Holy Spirit is the lifting power of the church of Christ.

Paul told us that we are *"clearly...an epistle of Christ...written not with ink but by the Spirit of the living God, not on tablets of stone but on tablets of flesh, that is, of the heart"* (2 Cor. 3:3). The Holy Spirit begins in the heart, right in the depths of human affections. He brings into the heart the riches of the revelation of Christ, implanting a purity and holiness there, so that out of the depths of the heart, praises well up continually.

The Holy Spirit will make us epistles of Christ, ever proclaiming that Jesus is our Lord and our Redeemer and that He is ever before God as a slain Lamb. God has never put away that revelation. Because of the perfect atonement of that slain Lamb, there is salvation, healing, and deliverance for all. Some people think that they have to be cleansed only once, but as we walk in the light, the blood of Jesus Christ is ever cleansing us (1 John 1:7).

The very life of Christ has been put within us and is moving within us—a perfect life. May the Lord help us to see the power of this life. The days of a man's life are seventy years (Ps. 90:10), and so in the natural order of things, my life will be finished in seven years. But I have begun a new life that will never end. *"From everlasting to everlasting, You are God"* (v. 2). This is the life I have come into, and there is no end to this life. In me is working a power that is stronger than every power. Christ, the power of God, is formed within me. I can see why we need to be clothed from above, for the life within me is a thousand times bigger than I am outside. There must be a tremendous expansion. I see, and cannot help seeing, that this life cannot be understood in the natural. No natural reason can comprehend the divine plan.

Our All-Sufficient God

We are not *"sufficient of ourselves to think of anything as being from ourselves, but our sufficiency is from God"* (2 Cor. 3:5). We have left the old order of things. If we go back, we miss the plan. We can never have confidence in the flesh (Phil. 3:3); we cannot touch that. We are in a new order, a spiritual order. It is a new life of absolute faith in our God's sufficiency in everything that pertains to our salvation.

You could never come into this place and be a Seventh-day Adventist, for the law has no place in you. You are set free from it. At the same time, like Paul, you are bound in the Spirit (Acts 20:22) so that you would not do anything to grieve the Lord.

Paul further told us that God has *"made us sufficient as ministers of the new covenant, not of the letter but of the Spirit; for the letter kills, but the Spirit gives life"* (2 Cor. 3:6). It is one thing to read this and another thing to have the revelation of it and to see the spiritual force of it. Any man can live in the letter and become dry and wordy, limited in knowledge of spiritual truths and spending all his time splitting hairs. But as soon as he touches the realm of the Spirit, dryness goes; the spirit of criticism leaves. There can be no divisions in a life in the Spirit. The Spirit of God brings such pliability and such love! There is no love like the love in the Spirit. It is a pure, holy, divine love that is poured out in our hearts by the Spirit (Rom. 5:5). It loves to serve and to honor the Lord.

The Holy Spirit's Life-Changing Power

I can never estimate what the baptism in the Holy Spirit has meant to me these past fifteen years. It seems as if every year has had three years packed into it, so that I feel as if I have had forty-five years of happy service since 1907. Life is getting better all the time. It is a luxury to be filled with the Spirit, and at the same time it is a divine command for us: *"Do not be drunk with wine, in which is dissipation; but be filled with the Spirit"* (Eph. 5:18). No Pentecostal person ought to get out of bed without being lost in the Spirit and speaking in tongues as the Spirit gives utterance. No one should come through the door of the church without speaking in tongues or having a psalm or a note of praise (1 Cor. 14:26).

Regarding the incoming of the Spirit, I emphasize that He should so fill us that every member in the body is yielded to Him. I also emphasize that no one is baptized in the Spirit without speaking in tongues as the Spirit gives utterance. I maintain that with a constant filling, you will speak in tongues morning, noon, and night. As you live in the Spirit, when you walk down the steps of your house, the Devil will have to flee before you. You will be more than a conqueror over the Devil (Rom. 8:37).

I see everything as a failure except what is done in the Spirit. But as you live in the Spirit, you move, act, eat, drink, and do everything to the glory of God (1 Cor. 10:31). Our message is always this: *"Be filled with the Spirit."* This is God's place for you, and it is as far above the natural life as the heavens are above the earth. Yield yourself so that God will fill you.

The Wonderful New Covenant

The Israelites tried Moses tremendously. They were always in trouble. But as he went up onto the mountain and God unfolded to him the Ten Commandments, the glory fell. He rejoiced to bring those two tablets of stone down from the mountain, and his very face shone with the glory. He was bringing to Israel that which, if obeyed, would bring life.

I think of my Lord coming from heaven. I think all heaven was moved by the sight. The letter of the law was brought by Moses, and it was made glorious, but all its glory was dimmed before the excelling glory that Jesus brought to us in the Spirit of life. The glory of Sinai paled before the glory of Pentecost. Those tablets of stone with their "Thou shalt not's" are done away with, for they never brought life to anyone. The Lord has brought in a new covenant, putting His law in our minds and writing it in our hearts (Jer. 31:33)—this new law of the Spirit of life. As the Holy Spirit comes in, He fills us with love and liberty, and we shout for joy, "Done away! Done away!" (See 2 Corinthians 3:11 KJV.) Henceforth, there is a new cry in our hearts: *"I delight to do Your will, O my God"* (Ps. 40:8). *"He takes away the first that He may establish the second"* (Heb. 10:9). In other words, He takes away *"the ministry of death, written and engraved on stones"* (2 Cor. 3:7), so that He may establish *"the ministry of righteousness"* (v. 9), this life in the Spirit.

You ask, "Does a man who is filled with the Spirit cease to keep the commandments?" I simply repeat what the Spirit of God has told us here, that this *"ministry of death, written and engraved on stones"* (and you know that the Ten Commandments were written on stones) is *"done away* [with]*"* (v. 11 KJV). However, the man who becomes a living epistle of Christ, written by the Spirit of the living God, has ceased to be an adulterer or a murderer or a covetous man; the will of God is his delight. I love to do the will of God; there is no irksomeness to it. It is no trial to pray, no trouble to read the Word of God; it is not a hard thing to go to the place of worship. With the psalmist I say, *"I was glad when they said to me, 'Let us go into the house of the LORD'"* (Ps. 122:1).

How does this new life work out? It works out because God *"works in you both to will and to do for His good pleasure"* (Phil. 2:13). There is a big difference between a pump and a spring. The law is a pump; the baptism in the Holy Spirit is a spring. The old pump gets out of order; the parts wear out, and the well runs dry. *"The letter kills"* (2 Cor. 3:6). But the spring is ever bubbling up, and there is a ceaseless flow direct from the throne of God. There is life.

It is written of Christ, *"You love righteousness and hate wickedness"* (Ps. 45:7). In this new life in the Spirit, in this new covenant life, you love the things that are right and pure and holy, and you shudder at all things that are wrong. Jesus was able to say, *"The ruler of this world is coming, and he has nothing in Me"* (John 14:30), and the moment we are filled with the Spirit of God, we are brought into a wonderful condition like this. Furthermore, as we continue to be filled with the Spirit, the Enemy cannot have an inch of territory in us.

How to Bring Conviction of Sin

Do you not believe that you can be so filled with the Spirit that a person who is not living right can be judged and convicted by your presence? As we go on in the life of the Spirit, it will be said of us that a vile person is convicted in our presence. Jesus lived in this realm and moved in it, and His life was a constant reproof to the wickedness around Him. "But He was the Son of God," you say. God, through Him, has brought us into the place of sonship, and I believe that if the Holy Spirit has a chance at us, He can make something of us and bring us to the same place.

I don't want to boast. If I glory in anything, it is only in the Lord, who has been so gracious to me (1 Cor. 1:31). But I remember a wonderful time of conviction. I stepped out of a railway coach to wash my hands. I had a season of prayer, and the Lord just filled me to overflowing with His love. I was going to a convention in Ireland, and I could not get there fast enough. As I returned to my seat, I believe that the Spirit of the Lord was so heavy upon me that my face must have shone. (When the Spirit transforms a man's very countenance, he cannot tell this on his own.) There were two clerical men sitting together, and as I got into the coach again, one of them cried out, "You convict me of sin." Within three minutes everyone in the coach was crying to God for salvation. This has happened many times in my life. It is the ministry of the Spirit that Paul spoke of. This filling of the Spirit will make your life effective, so that even the people in the stores where you shop will want to leave your presence because they are brought under conviction.

We must move away from everything that pertains to the letter. All that we do must be done under the anointing of the Spirit. Our problem has been that we as Pentecostal people have been living in the letter. Believe what the Holy Spirit said through Paul—that this entire *"ministry of condemnation"* (2 Cor. 3:9) that has hindered your liberty in Christ is done away with. The law has been done away with! As far as you are concerned, that old order of things is forever done away with, and the Spirit of God has brought in a new life of purity and love. The Holy Spirit takes it for granted that you are finished with all the things of the old life when you become a new creation in Christ. In the life in the Spirit, the old allurements have lost their power. The Devil will meet you at every turn, but the Spirit of God will always *"lift up a standard against him"* (Isa. 59:19).

Oh, if God had His way, we would be like torches, purifying the very atmosphere wherever we go, moving back the forces of wickedness.

> *An Interpretation of Tongues:* "'The Lord is that Spirit.' He moves in your heart. He shows you that the power within you is mightier than all the powers of darkness."

What do I mean when I say that the law has been done away with? Do I mean that you will be disloyal? No, you will be more than loyal. Will you grumble when you are treated badly? No, you will turn the other cheek (Matt. 5:39). You will always do this when God lives in you. Leave yourself in God's hands. Enter into rest. *"For he who has entered His rest has himself also ceased from his works as God did from His"* (Heb. 4:10). Oh, this is a lovely rest! The whole life is a Sabbath. This is the only life that can glorify God. It is a life of joy, and every day is a day of heaven on earth.

Daily Transformation

There is a continual transformation in this life. Beholding the Lord and His glory, we are *"transformed into the same image from glory to glory, just as by the Spirit of the Lord"* (2 Cor. 3:18). There is a continual unveiling, a constant revelation, a repeated clothing from above. I want you to promise God never to look back, never to go back to what the Spirit has said is done away with. I promised the Lord that I would never allow myself to doubt His Word.

There is one thing about a baby: he takes all that comes to him. A so-called prudent man lets his reason cheat him out of God's best. But a baby takes all the milk his mother brings and even tries to swallow the bottle. The baby can't walk, but the mother carries him; the baby can't dress himself, but the mother dresses him. The baby can't even talk. Similarly, in the life of the Spirit, God undertakes to do what we cannot do. We are carried along by Him. He clothes us, and He gives us utterance. Oh, that we all had the simplicity of babes!

Ten

Greater Works Than These

 want all you people to have a good time, all to be at ease, all to be without pain. I want all to be free. There is a man here with great pain in his head. I am going to lay my hands on him in the name of Jesus, and he will tell you what God has done. I believe it is the right thing to do, before I begin preaching to you, to help this poor man so that he will enjoy the meeting like us, without any pain.

(The man referred to had his head wrapped up in a bandage and was in pain. After he was prayed for, he testified that he had no pain.)

God's Blessings Available to All

I want you all to be in a place where you receive much blessing from God. It is impossible for any of you to leave with pain if you would only believe God. If you receive the Word of God tonight, it will give life to you; it gives deliverance to every captive. I want to preach the Word tonight so that all the people will know the truth. You will leave with a knowledge of the deliverance of God.

I want everyone to receive a blessing at the start of the meeting. Not one person needs to live outside of the plan of God. If you have pain in your knee, and if you believe when you stand up, you will definitely be free. I believe the Word of God. God has promised that if we will believe, we can have whatever we ask (Matt. 21:22).

I want you to be blessed now. I find I get blessed as I ask—on the street, everywhere! If you find me on the street or anywhere else, if I am alone, I will be talking to God. I make it my business to talk to God all the time. If I wake in the night, I make it my business to pray, and I believe that's the reason that God keeps me right, always right, always ready. I believe that God the Holy Spirit keeps us living in communion with God. I want you to begin now; begin talking to God.

Jesus is the Way and the Truth (John 14:6); therefore, all that Jesus said was true. Jesus said, *"Most assuredly, I say to you, he who believes in Me, the works that I do he will do also; and greater works than these he will do, because I go to My Father"* (v. 12). Has He gone? Yes, He has gone to the Father.

Send the Light

Do you see this electric light? This light is receiving power from the power plant; it has a receiver and transmitter. The power plant may be a mile or two away. The wires that are conveying the current to and from are covered. We are getting the light from the bare wire underneath; the power is passing through the bare wire and giving us light.

I want you to understand the life in Christ. Jesus sends the light—He sends His life through the light—and it illuminates the life and then returns. And just as you are holy inside, your life becomes full of illumination. My life is from Him, my life goes back to Him, and I am kept by the life of God.

I touch people, and instantly they are changed. The life of the Son of God goes through and passes on. I live by the faith of the Son of God (Gal. 2:20).

What Does It Mean to Believe?

"He who believes in Me" (John 14:12). *"He who believes."* The devils believe and tremble (James 2:19). In the same way, people follow Scripture as if it had nothing to do with their lives. The Scriptures may be life or letter. What is the Word? It is spirit and life-giving when we believe (John 6:63). What is believing? Believing is the asking of the divine life that God gives. Who desires this? Everyone in this place can have divine life.

I do not believe in baptismal regeneration. Nor can you be saved by riches. Jesus says, *"You must be born again"* (John 3:7). The new birth comes through faith in the Lord Jesus Christ, and you can be saved in a field as well as in a church. The heart is the key. When the heart desires righteousness, God makes Himself known. I want you to be saved by the blood tonight. Someone is saying, "I want to be saved." Shall I bring you to the Word? *"Everyone who asks receives"* (Matt. 7:8). Who says this? Jesus says this. *"Everyone who asks receives."*

> If I ask Him to receive me
> Will He say me nay?
> Not till earth and not till heaven
> Pass away.

A New Song

"Salvation is of the LORD" (Jonah 2:9). No man can save you; no man can heal you. If anyone has been healed in these meetings, it is the Lord who has healed him.

I would not claim under any circumstances that I can heal anybody, but I believe God's Word. *"He who believes in Me...greater works than these he will do, because I go to My Father"* (John 14:12). He is lovely. Lovely Jesus.

> He knows it all, He knows it all,
>> My Father knows it all.
> The bitter tears how fast they fall,
>> He knows, my Father knows it all.

Isn't He lovely? If you get saved tonight, you will have another song:

> He knows it all, He knows it all,
>> My Father knows it all.
> The joy that comes that overflows
>> He knows, my Father knows it all.

Before I was baptized in the Holy Spirit, there were many songs that I sang only as they were written. God began a change, and He changed many songs. I believe God wants to change the song in your heart. He changed the following song for me. This is how it is sung:

> Oh, then it will be glory for me,
>> It will be glory for me.

But God changed it:

> Oh, it is now glory for me,
> It is now glory for me.
> As now by His grace I can look on His face,
> Now it is glory, glory for me.

I want you to have your tune changed. The present-tense songs are better than the future-tense songs. If you get a full salvation, you will have a present-tense song. Sometimes it is a good thing to be able to hope for something, but it is a better thing to have it.

I used to hope and trust that I would be baptized in the Holy Spirit. But when I spoke in tongues—no, when He spoke!—then I knew I was baptized. When you get baptized in the Holy Spirit, the Spirit speaks through you. Then you know that the Comforter has come.

Has He come to you? Has the Comforter come to you? You must have Him. You must be filled with the Spirit; you must have an overflowing. Jesus says, *"You shall receive power when the Holy Spirit has come upon you"* (Acts 1:8). I want you to have power.

The Wonderful Words of Jesus

Let's look at the following Scripture: *"Whatever you ask in My name, that I will do, that the Father may be glorified in the Son"* (John 14:13). If we ask anything in His name, He will do it! Who says this? Jesus—that blessed Jesus, that lovely Jesus, that Incarnation from heaven, that blessed Son of God. How He wants to bless! How He saves *"to the uttermost"*

(Heb. 7:25)! No one has ever spoken as He spoke (John 7:46). What did He say? *"Come to Me, all you who labor and are heavy laden, and I will give you rest"* (Matt. 11:28). Hear what else Jesus says about Himself: *"For God did not send His Son into the world to condemn the world, but that the world through Him might be saved"* (John 3:17). How beautiful! Jesus wants us all to be saved.

Have you ever looked at Jesus in His sadness? Just take a look at Him on the Mount of Olives, looking over Jerusalem, weeping and saying, *"O Jerusalem, Jerusalem...How often I wanted to gather your children together, as a hen gathers her chicks under her wings, but you were not willing!"* (Matt. 23:37). Shall it be said of you, *"How often I wanted to gather* [you], *as a hen gathers her chicks under her wings, but you were not willing"*? Will you come to Him?

Hear what He said: ***"Whatever you ask in My name, that I will do"*** (John 14:13, emphasis added). What do you want? How much do you want? Do you want anything? Are you thirsty? Jesus says, "Come to Me, all who thirst, and I will give you the water of life." (See Revelation 22:17.) Are you hungry? He who eats the flesh and drinks the blood of the Son of Man will live forever (John 6:54).

Do you want to live forever? Jesus saves *"to the uttermost"* (Heb. 7:25). He heals. He helps all who come to Him.

How many are coming for healing? How many are coming for salvation? Listen. *"Whatever you ask in My name, that I will do"* (John 14:13). This is the Word of the living God, the Son of God. How beautifully God speaks of Jesus! *"This is my beloved Son"*

(Matt. 3:17). Yet Jesus gave Himself for us. He gave Himself as a ransom for us.

How many are going to receive Him? Take the water of life freely. You may ask, "How can I receive Him?" *"Believe on the Lord Jesus Christ, and you will be saved"* (Acts 16:31). Jesus said, *"He who hears My word and believes in Him who sent Me has everlasting life"* (John 5:24).

Who were the people who followed Jesus? Those who loved Him in their hearts. Do you love Him in your heart? From this day, if you do love Him, you will begin to hate all kinds of sin, and you will love all kinds of righteousness. That is the secret. The man who says he loves God but truly loves the world is a liar. God says that *"the truth is not in him"* (1 John 2:4). *"If anyone loves the world, the love of the Father is not in him"* (v. 15). You can tell tonight whether you love God or not. Do you love the world? Then the love of the Father is not in you. If you hate the world, the love of the Lord Jesus is in you. Hallelujah!

I want to make you love Him. Is He worth loving? What has He done? He bought salvation. He died to deliver. *"The wages of sin is death, but the gift of God is eternal life"* (Rom. 6:23).

I leave the decision with you. Will you love Him? Will you serve Him? Will you? He knows it. He understands.

> There's no one that loves me like Jesus;
> > There's no one that knows me like Him.
> He knows all your trials, He knows all your sickness;
> > There's no one that knows me like Him.

"Come to Me" (Matt. 11:28). That's what Jesus says. He knows you are needy.

Eleven

The Faith That Delivers

*By faith Enoch was taken away so that he
did not see death, "and was not found, because
God had taken him"; for before he was taken he had
this testimony, that he pleased God. But without faith
it is impossible to please Him, for he who comes to
God must believe that He is.*
—Hebrews 11:5–6

elieve that God is able to work out His plan in your life. He will work mightily through you if you believe. Great possibilities are within your reach if you dare to believe.

Evil spirits can have no more control if I believe that God is, that He is living and active. I do believe! I know I am free from all the powers of darkness, free from all the powers of evil, and it is a wonderful thing to be free. Christ said, *"You shall know the truth, and the truth shall make you free"* (John 8:32). Because you are free, you step into the freedom of liberated men and claim the possessions of God.

Dare to Believe

This is the dispensation of the Holy Spirit. It has been thirty-three years since God filled me with the Holy Spirit. The fire burned in my bones then, and it is still burning, producing more activity for God than thirty-three years ago. The Holy Spirit's supply has not been exhausted.

God is waiting for people who dare to believe, and when you believe, *"all things are possible"* (Mark 9:23).

> Only believe, only believe;
>> All things are possible, only believe.
> Only believe, only believe;
>> All things are possible, only believe.

God wants to sweep away all unbelief from your heart. He wants you to dare to believe His Word. It is the Word of the Spirit. If you allow anything to come between you and the Word, it will poison your whole system, and you will have no hope. One bit of unbelief against the Word is poison. It is like the Devil putting a spear into you. The Word of Life is the breath of heaven, the life-giving power by which your very self is changed. By it, you begin to bear the image of the heavenly One.

Miracles in South Africa

A young man in South Africa, who was dying of tuberculosis, read one of my books. He got saved, and then God healed him. This young man grew so much in the knowledge of God that he was made a pastor. When I arrived in South Africa five years ago, he came up to me like a son to a father and said, "If you like, I will go with you all over South Africa." He bought the best car for the job. If you go to South Africa, you must have a car that can go through the plowed fields, one that will handle rough terrain and wet conditions. That young man drove me many miles through all the territories, right among the Zulus, and God took us through everything. Talk about life! Why, this is overcoming life!

When I arrived in Cape Town, a man was there whose deathly face was filled with the very Devil's manifestation of cancer. I said to the people, "There is a man in this place suffering tremendously. He does not even know I am talking about him. I give you the choice. If you want me to deliver that man so that he can enjoy the meeting, I will go down in the name of the Lord and deliver him, or I will preach." They said, "Come down." I went down, and the people saw what God can do. They saw that man shouting and raving, for he was like an intoxicated man. He was shouting, "I was bound, but I am free!" It was a wonderful thing to see that man changed.

One man, after spending $4,500 on his wife for operation after operation, year after year, brought her helpless to the meeting. I went to her and said, "Look here, this is the greatest opportunity of your life. I will give an altar call tonight. Fifty people will come up, and when you see them loosed, believe, and you will be loosed like them. Then we will have a testimony from you." They came, and I laid my hands upon them in the name of the Lord. I said, "Testify," and they testified. This woman saw their faces, and when all these people were through, I asked her, "Do you believe?" She said, "I cannot help but believe." There is something in the manifestation of faith.

I laid my hands upon her in the name of Jesus, and the power of God went right through her. I said, "In the name of Jesus, arise and walk." An impossibility? If you do not venture out in faith, you remain ordinary as long as you live. If you dare the impossible, God will abundantly do far above all you ask or think (Eph. 3:20).

As if a cannon had blown her into the air, she rose. I thought her husband would go mad with joy and excitement because he saw his wife mightily moved and made free by the power of God. She was in the first meeting afterward to glorify God.

Wonderful Jesus!

The divine plan is so much greater than all human thought. When we are willing to yield to His sovereign will, when we have no reserve, how wonderful God is. He is always willing to open the door until our whole lives are filled with the fragrance of heaven.

Jesus is the substance and fullness of the divine nature (Col. 2:9), and He dwells in our hearts. Oh, this wonderful, fascinating Jesus! What a wonderful Jesus we have! Something about Him kindles fire in the darkest place. Something about our Lord makes all darkness light. When we have Him, we have more than we can speak or think about. God's Son can set the world ablaze and bring heaven right into the place where we live. Dare to believe God, and *"nothing will be impossible for you"* (Matt. 17:20).

Twelve

The Ministry of the Flaming Sword

his glorious inworking of Holy Spirit power is preparing us for rapture. Our greatest theme is the glory of the splendor of our Lord—His face, His tenderness, His sweetness! He makes our hearts long to be forever with Him. Amen! Let it be so!

What then shall we say to these things? If God is for us, who can be against us?...Who shall separate us from the love of Christ? Shall tribulation, or distress, or persecution, or famine, or nakedness, or peril, or sword?...Yet in all these things we are more than conquerors through Him who loved us. For I am persuaded that neither death nor life, nor angels nor principalities nor powers, nor things present nor things to come, nor height nor depth, nor any other created thing, shall be able to separate us from the love of God which is in Christ Jesus our Lord. (Rom. 8:31, 35, 37–39)

Oh, the joy of the thought of this! *"Who shall separate us from the love of Christ?"* (Rom. 8:35). This is a place of confidence, assurance, and rest, where God has perfect control over all human weakness. You stand as if on the Mount of Transfiguration, manifested and glorified in the presence of God. You are able to say, "I know all things are working together for good within me" (see Romans 8:28); all that can be destroyed is silently being destroyed so that He can have preeminence in your body. *"If God is for us, who can be against us?"* (v. 31).

God is bringing forth a new creation. The sons of God are to be manifested, and you must see your inheritance in the Holy Spirit. Nothing can separate you from Christ's love (vv. 38–39)! What is it God wants you to know? Right in your earthly temple, God has brought forth a son with power, with manifestation, with grace, crowned already in the earth, crowned with glory. *"The glory which You gave Me I have given them, that they may be one just as We are one"* (John 17:22).

The Spirit of the Lord is showing me that God must get a people who can see that from before the foundation of the world, He has had them in mind. (See Ephesians 1:4.) God has been delivering us through all difficulty. Where sin abounded, He has brought in His grace (Rom. 5:20). Where disease came in to steal our lives, God raised up a standard. We have come through tribulation. God has been purifying us, strengthening us, equipping us with divine boldness by His almighty power, until we can say, *"What then shall we say to these things? If God is for us, who can be against us?"* (Rom. 8:31).

Should we dethrone what we know has equipped us and brought us through to the present? Should we allow our hearts to fail us in the day of adversity? No! God has already strengthened and perfected! Weakness has been made strong! Corruption has been changed to purity! In tribulation the fire of God has purified us. *"What then shall we say to these things?"* (Rom. 8:31). *"Our light affliction...is working for us a far more exceeding and eternal weight of glory"* (2 Cor. 4:17).

The Power of the New Creation

People have been in meetings where the glory of God has fallen, where the fingerprints of God have been upon everything, and where fortifications have been made in the body. The next morning the power of Satan has attacked them. Why does this happen? The spiritual life, the Son manifested, the glory of the new creation, is already in our mortal bodies, but the flesh, being a battleground for the Enemy, is tested. But what God is forming is greater than the mortal body, for the spirit that is awakening to the glorious liberty of a child of God is greater. *"What then shall we say?"* How can we compare this with what is to come?

"It is the Spirit who gives life; the flesh profits nothing" (John 6:63). Though *"worms destroy this body"* (Job 19:26 KJV), I have a life greater than this life that will look upon God, that will see Him in His perfection, that will behold Him in His glory, that will be changed to be like Him. By the presence of God, a new creation will so clothe us that we will be like Him. Knowing this, should I give place to the

Devil? Should I fear? Should I let my feelings change the experience of the Word of God? Should I trust in my fears? No! A million times, no! There has never been any good thing in the flesh (Rom. 7:18), but God has given life to the spirit until we live a new life divine and are eternally shaped for God.

"What then shall we say?" (Rom. 8:31). Are you going to let the past, in which God Himself has worked for you, bring you to a place of distress? Or are you standing during your testing, quoting God's Word—*"Now we are children of God"* (1 John 3:2)—and remembering how God has answered your prayers, brought light into your home, delivered you from carnality, and touched you when no power in the world could help? *"What then shall we say?"* *"Who shall lay any thing to the charge of God's elect?"* (Rom. 8:33 KJV). *"I know whom I have believed"* (2 Tim. 1:12), and I am persuaded that He who purposed us for God will surely bring us to the place where we will receive the crown of life through the faith that God has given us. God is in you and is mightily forming within you a new creation by the Spirit in order to make you ready for the glory that will be revealed in Him.

Someone said to me the other day, "I am in terrible trouble; a man is cursing me all the time." *"If God is for us, who can be against us?"* (Rom. 8:31). God is never tightfisted with any of His blessings. He takes you into all He has. *"He who did not spare His own Son...how shall He not with Him also freely give us all things?"* (v. 32). God has given us Jesus, the heart of His love, *"the express image of His person"* (Heb. 1:3), perfect in brilliance, purity, righteousness, and glory. I have seen Him many times, and seeing Him always changes me. Victory over your struggle is one of the *"all things"* (Rom. 8:32). Many needs have broken my heart, but I could say to the troubled one, "God is greater than your heart, greater than your circumstances, greater than the thing that holds you. God will deliver you if you dare to believe Him." But I have to emphasize it again and again and again before I can get the people to believe God.

A dear woman was marvelously delivered and saved, but she said, "I am addicted to smoking. What shall I do?" "Oh," I said, "smoke night and day." She said, "In our circumstances, we take a glass of wine, and it has a hold on me." "Oh," I said, "drink all you can." It brought some solace to her, but she was still in misery. She said, "We play cards." I said, "Play on!" But after being saved, she called her maid and said, "Wire to London and stop the shipment of those cigarettes." The new life does not want these things. It has no desire for them. The old is dethroned.

A clergyman came to me. He said, "I have a terrible craving for tobacco." I said, "Is it the old man or the new?" He broke down. "I know it's the old," he said. *"Put off the old man with his deeds"* (Col. 3:9).

Someone told me, "I have an unlawful affection for another." I said, "You need revelation. Since God has given you Jesus, He will give you all things. He will give you power over the thing, and it will be broken." And God broke it.

Allow God to touch your flesh. He has given life to your spirit. Allow Him to reign, for He will reign until all is subdued. He is King in your life and is preeminent over your affections, your will, your desires, your plans. He rules as Lord of Hosts over you, in you, and through you, to chasten you and bring you to the perfection of your desired haven. *"Christ in you* [is] *the hope of glory"* (Col. 1:27). *"Who shall separate us from the love of Christ?"* (Rom. 8:35). Once things could separate us, but no more. We have a vision. What is the vision? Those days when we have eaten of *"the hidden manna"* (Rev. 2:17).

The Benefit of the Flaming Sword

When I was baptized in the Holy Spirit, God showed me a wonderful truth. After Adam and Eve transgressed and were driven out of the Garden, the Tree of Life was guarded by a flaming sword—a sword of death if they entered the Garden. But the baptism in the Holy Spirit put the Tree of Life right inside of me and a flaming sword right outside of me to keep the Devil from me, so that I can eat the eternal bread all the time. I am eating this wonderful bread of life. Nothing can separate us from this life. It is increasing tremendously, perpetually. Rapture has something to do with it.

"[What] *shall separate us?"* (Rom. 8:35). Tribulations come, but they only press us closer to persecution—the finest thing that can come. Among the persecuted you find those who are the ripest, the holiest, the purest, the most intent, those who are the most filled with divine order. All these things work together for our good (v. 28). Nothing comes except what is helpful. Trials lift you. Distresses give you a sigh, but God causes you to triumph. *"Greater is he that is in you"* (1 John 4:4 KJV) than all the powers of darkness.

Whatever befalls you as you abide in Him is the good hand of God upon you so that you won't lose your inheritance. Every trial is a boost, every burden a place of exchanging strength. God will work. *"Who shall lay any thing to the charge of God's elect?"* (Rom. 8:33 KJV). People do it, but it makes no difference; *"God is for us"* (v. 31). *"'Eye has not seen, nor ear heard, nor have entered into the heart of man the things which God has prepared for those who love Him.' But God has revealed them to us through His Spirit"* (1 Cor. 2:9–10). *"No weapon formed against you shall prosper"* (Isa. 54:17).

Know the wisdom and purpose of God's great hand upon you. Glorify God in distresses and persecution, for the Spirit of God is made manifest in these situations. Be chastened! Be perfected! Press on to heights, depths, breadths. Faith is the victory (1 John 5:4). The hope is within you (1 Pet. 3:15). The joy is set before you (Heb. 12:2). God gives the peace that passes all understanding (Phil. 4:7). We know that the flesh has withered in the presence of the purifying of the Word. He who has brought you to this point will take you to the end. I have mourned and wept bitterly when I needed revelation from God, but I did not need to do so.

The Lord lifts up and changes and operates. He remakes body and soul until He can say, "There is no spot in you." Yes, it was persecution, tribulation, and distress that drew us near to Him. These places of trial were places of uplifting, places of change, where God operated by the Spirit. Do not bypass this way, but let God have His way.

God stretched out His hand, covered us with the mantle of His love, and brought us nearer and nearer to the channel of His grace. Then our hearts moved and yielded and so turned to the Lord that every moment has seen a divine place where God has met us and stretched out His arms and said, *"Seek My face"* (Ps. 27:8); *"look to Me"* (Isa. 45:22). Behold what great love the Master has for you, to lead you to the fountain of living water. Yield! Be led! Let God be glorified! Amen.

Thirteen

Launch Out

So it was, as the multitude pressed about Him to hear the word of God, that He stood by the Lake of Gennesaret, and saw two boats standing by the lake; but the fishermen had gone from them and were washing their nets. Then He got into one of the boats, which was Simon's, and asked him to put out a little from the land. And He sat down and taught the multitudes from the boat. When He had stopped speaking, He said to Simon, "Launch out into the deep and let down your nets for a catch." But Simon answered and said to Him, "Master, we have toiled all night and caught nothing; nevertheless at Your word I will let down the net." And when they had done this, they caught a great number of fish, and their net was breaking. So they signaled to their partners in the other boat to come and help them. And they came and filled both the boats, so that they began to sink. When Simon Peter saw it, he fell down at Jesus' knees, saying, "Depart from me, for I am a sinful man, O Lord!" For he and all who were with him were astonished at the catch of fish which they had taken; and so also were James and John, the

sons of Zebedee, who were partners with Simon. And
Jesus said to Simon, "Do not be afraid.
From now on you will catch men."
—Luke 5:1–10

 very time I preach I am impressed with the fact that the Word of God is full of life and vitality, and it changes us. God's Word must come to pass in us.

How can we get more faith? God's Word tells us, *"Faith comes by hearing, and hearing by the word of God"* (Rom. 10:17). Faith is a gift. We receive our inheritance by faith. We are spiritual children— *"children of God without fault"* (Phil. 2:15). May God manifest this in us by the power of His might.

The people said to Jesus, *"Blessed is the womb that bore You"* (Luke 11:27). But Jesus said, *"Blessed are those who hear the word of God and keep it!"* (v. 28). This blessed Christ of God! They said, *"'No man ever spoke like this Man!'"* (John 7:46). He does not speak as the scribes speak; He teaches us as one having authority." (See Matthew 7:29.)

The living Son of God—the Son of His love— came to us with understanding, ministering the breath of His Father. We knew a life-giving Spirit. The moment we believed, we had a new nature, a new life. Jesus had a wonderful word, a sweet influence. Men saw love in those beautiful eyes and were convicted of sin in His presence.

A Remarkable Catch

The people crowded around Jesus, and He sat in a boat and taught them. Then Jesus said to Peter,

"Launch out into the deep and let down your nets for a catch" (Luke 5:4). Peter answered, *"We have toiled all night and caught nothing"* (v. 5). Perhaps he was thinking, "Lord, You know nothing about fishing. Daytime is the wrong time to fish." But he said, *"Nevertheless at Your word I will let down the net"* (v. 5). I believe every fish in the lake tried to get into that net. They wanted to see Jesus. I must see Jesus.

Peter filled one ship, then another. Oh, what would happen if you lowered all the nets? Believe God! He says, *"Look to **Me**, and be saved"* (Isa. 45:22, emphasis added). He says, *"Come to Me, all you who labor and are heavy laden, and I will give you rest"* (Matt. 11:28). He says, *"He who believes in Me has everlasting life"* (John 6:47). Believe! Oh, believe! It is the Word of God. *"There is a river whose streams shall make glad the city of God"* (Ps. 46:4).

Peter saw the ship sinking. He looked around and saw Jesus. He fell down at Jesus' feet, saying, *"Depart from me, for I am a sinful man, O Lord!"* (Luke 5:8). He and all who were with him were astonished at the number of fish that they had caught. That spotless Lamb stood there. *"They looked to Him and were radiant, and their faces were not ashamed"* (Ps. 34:5).

To see Jesus is to see a new way, to see all things differently. It means a new life and new plans. As we gaze at Him, we are satisfied; there is none like Him. Sin moves away.

Jesus was the express image of the Father (Heb. 1:3). The Father could not be in the midst, so He clothed Jesus with a body—with eternal resources. Let us gather together unto Him. Let us move toward Him. He has all we need. He will fulfill the desires of our hearts, granting all our petitions.

A Cripple and a Cancer Patient

There was a banquet for cripples, and in the middle of it a father brought a boy on his shoulder and lifted the boy up. I said, "In the name of Jesus." The boy said, "Papa! Papa! It is going all over me." Jesus healed him.

There was a man who had cancer in the rectum. Night and day he had morphine every ten minutes. I went to see him. He said, "I do not know how to believe God! Oh, if only I could believe. Oh, if only God would work a miracle." I placed my hand upon him in Jesus' name. I said to the nurse, "You go to the other room. God will work a miracle." The Spirit of God came upon me. In the name of Jesus I laid hold of the evil power, with hatred in my heart against the power of Satan. While I was praying, he was healed. I said to the nurse, "Come in." She did not understand, but the man knew that God had done it.

Previously, this man had had a hobby; it was yachting. He had been very fond of his yacht; it had been all he had wanted to talk about. Did he want to talk about yachting now? No! He said, "Tell me about Jesus—the Sin-Bearer—the Lamb of God."

He who made things happen—will you let Him in?

The Importance of Communion, God's Word, and Prayer

In Christ, we are one body. The bread and the wine represent Christ. (See 1 Corinthians 11:23–26.) His body was *"broken for you"* (1 Cor. 11:24), broken to meet every human need.

"The word of God is living and powerful" (Heb. 4:12). How it works in spirit, soul, and body, separating the desires, heart, thought, word, deed, and intent! The Word enters into the *"joints and marrow"* (v. 12). It is the Word of the living God.

The Lord says, "Begin to pray if you want the furniture of God's place put in order." You kneel down; you begin to pray. You begin in the Spirit; the Spirit leads you to pray by the Spirit. As you begin, God will come in. God will lift you as you begin.

I am here to help you to a place of beginnings. You must begin. Come to a Person who has no end—Jesus. Feed upon Him; believe Him. The day is a day of communion. One body means unbroken fellowship. Look at Him. Reign with Him. Live in His presence.

> Peace, peace, sweet peace;
> Sweet peace—the gift of God's love.

God could give us many gifts, but God is satisfied with the lovely gift of Him who suffered and died for us. Keep the vision of one bread and one body.

Bring your ships to land. Forsake all, and follow Him. Peter was astonished, and all who were with him, at the catch of fish that they had taken. Jesus said to Peter, *"Do not be afraid. From now on you will catch men"* (Luke 5:10).

Fourteen

The Moving Breath
of the Spirit

he Word is God Himself. *"In the beginning was the Word, and the Word was with God, and the Word was God"* (John 1:1). Herein lies our attitude of rest. All our hope is in the Word of the living God. The Word of God *"abides forever"* (1 Pet. 1:23). Oh, the glorious truths found in His Word. Never compare this Book with other books. The Bible is from heaven. It does not contain the Word of God; it is the Word of God. It is supernatural in origin, eternal in duration, infinite in scope, and divine in authorship. Read it through; pray it in; write it down. *"The fear of the LORD is the beginning of wisdom"* (Ps. 111:10).

The knowledge of our weakness brought the greatness of redemption; knowledge is coupled with joy! You cannot have the knowledge of the Lord without joy. Rejoice in the knowledge of Him. Faith is peace. Not long petitions but faith is peace. Where faith is undisturbed, there is peace. I am speaking of eternal faith, daring to believe what God has said. If I dare to trust Him, I find that what He has said always comes to pass. We must not doubt. *"He who doubts is like a wave of the sea driven and tossed by the wind. For let not that man suppose that he will receive anything from the Lord"* (James 1:6–7). Have faith in God. *"Only believe"* (Mark 5:36).

The Blessedness of Being Filled

"Jesus, being filled with the Holy Spirit, returned from the Jordan" (Luke 4:1). Bringing out of the shadow the reality of the substance, the One who had been promised had come. He, our glorious Lord who could speak like no other, had come to help the oppressed. Jesus, I'll go through with You.

What does the Bible mean when it says, *"Be filled with the Spirit"* (Eph. 5:18)? Oh, what a difference when we understand Acts 2 and know the flow of the life of the Spirit! How the Word is illuminated! We leap for joy.

> *An Interpretation of Tongues:* "The King unfolds His will covering His child, flooding the soul with open vision, untiring zeal. Fire! Fire! Fire!—burning intensely in the human soul, until he becomes an expression of the King."

I know the Lord laid His hand on me. He filled me with the Holy Spirit.

This Jesus, this wonder-working Jesus, came to be King. Is He King? He must reign. Oh, to yield so that He always has the first place. Glory be to God! The Holy Spirit has come to abide forever, flooding our souls, for Jesus said, *"If I depart, I will send Him to you"* (John 16:7).

Has He come to you?
Has He come to you?
Has the Comforter come to you?

"When He [the Comforter] *has come, He will convict the world of sin"* (John 16:8). In Him God has enriched us and given us a perfection of revelation. The Holy Spirit came to fill the body and to bring forth what all the prophets had spoken of. Jesus said concerning the Holy Spirit, *"He will glorify Me, for He will take of what is Mine and declare it to you"* (v. 14).

The woman had a well (see John 4:5–14), but after the Holy Spirit came, it was a river, *"rivers of living water"* (John 7:38), giving life, giving truth, giving prophetic utterance. There was a divine incoming, *"fill*[ing] *with all the fullness of God"* (Eph. 3:19).

The baptism in the Holy Spirit is like a flash of lightning; it opens up divine revelation so that we can dance and sing in the Spirit, enjoying sweeter music and stronger character. *"Christ in you* [is] *the hope of glory"* (Col. 1:27). The baptism in the Holy Spirit brings us a vision of *"the glory of God in the face of Jesus Christ"* (2 Cor. 4:6). *"Jesus* [was] *filled with the Holy Spirit"* (Luke 4:1).

An Interpretation of Tongues: "He is the Spirit of Truth unveiling, making manifest, breathing through in such a way, burning, quickening, until men cry out, 'What must we do to be saved?' The breath of life burns with intensity until the world feels the warmth and cries, 'What must we do?'"

Oh, the joy of being filled with the Holy Spirit, with divine purpose! Oh, the satisfaction of being active *"in season and out of season"* (2 Tim. 4:2) with the sense of divine approval. As the apostles were in their day, so we are to be in our day: *"filled with all the fullness of God"* (Eph. 3:19). We are to have this same Holy Spirit, this same warmth, this same life, this same heaven in the soul. The Holy Spirit brings heaven to us as He reveals Jesus, who is the King of heaven. Oh, the perfection of belonging to Him. It prepares us for every need. He holds us in the divine moments. There is no need to groan, cry, agonize, or sigh.

"The Spirit of the Lord is upon [me]" (Luke 4:18)—the sense of the Holy Spirit, the knowledge of His power, the sweetness of His experience, the wonder of His presence, honoring the Word, making all new, meeting the present need. These are the last days. Very wonderful are they. They are blessed with mighty signs. The breath of the Spirit is unfolding, helping. I believe in the Holy Spirit. God gave us the Holy Spirit for true Sonlikeness.

The Mighty Moving of the Spirit in Sweden

In a park in Sweden, a large platform was erected for meetings on the condition that I did not lay my hands on the people. I said, "Lord, You know all about this. You can work." And there the Lord revealed His presence and healed and saved the people. I said, "Who here is in need? Put your hands up." Hands went up all over. I saw a large woman. I said, "Tell your trouble!" She said pains were all over her body. She was in terrible distress. I said,

"Lift up your hands in Jesus' name!" (Jesus came to heal the sick, to unbind, to set free. He said in John 14:12, *"He who believes in Me, the works that I do he will do also; and greater works than these he will do."*) I said, "In the name of Jesus, I set you free." Then I asked, "Are you free?" She replied, "Yes, perfectly free!"

Although I could not put my hands on the people, God put *His* hands on the people. God has wonderful ways of meeting the need. I believe I will see the glory of God setting people free from all weakness. Jesus said, *"The Spirit of the LORD is upon Me"* (Luke 4:18). He said to *"make disciples of all the nations"* (Matt. 28:19).

When I first preached this glorious truth in New Zealand, I saw hundreds baptized. But in Sweden some churches were not pleased. A woman in the king's household was healed; nevertheless, I had to leave the country.

Bountiful Blessings

On one occasion, I stayed on a side street. I arrived at 9:30 in the morning. The meeting was at 4:30, so I went to the coast for a few hours' rest. When I came back, the street was full from one end to the other with wheelchairs and cars filled with the helpless and needy. The people in charge said, "What are we going to do?" I said, "The Holy Spirit came to abide, to reign in supreme royal dignity. Live in freedom, anointing, inspiration, like a river flowing. Settle for nothing less, so that God may be glorified." God loosed the people and brought deliverance to the captives. Was that all? No, it was only the beginning! The house was packed, too! Oh, the joy of being ready! God must set us all on fire. There is much land to be possessed. The fields are ripe for harvest (John 4:35).

Oh, the cry of the people! Talk about weeping! Oh, the joy of weeping. You are in an awful place when you cannot weep when the breath of God is upon you. I continued helping the people. Oh, the breath of the Spirit. Jesus said, *"The Spirit of the LORD is upon Me"* (Luke 4:18). God spoke to me as clearly as could be, saying, "Ask Me! I'll give you all in the place." I thought this was something too big, but He whispered again, "Ask; I will give you all in the house." I said, "O my God, say it again." "Ask of Me. I will give you all in the house." I said, "I ask! I ask in faith! I believe it!" The breath of heaven filled the place. The people continued to fall down, weeping, crying, repenting.

There is something wonderful in this breath of heaven. Jesus said, *"The Spirit of the LORD is upon Me."* I repeat, *"Upon Me!"* May God move our hearts to act in this anointing. Do you want God to have you in His splendid palace? Is it the longing of your heart to come to this place? God can choose only those filled to the utmost. How many long to step into line, filled to the utmost, hungering and thirsting after God's fullness? Stand in a living experience as Jesus did, saying, *"The Spirit of the Lord is upon* [me]." May God grant it to every one of you. Amen.

Fifteen

Healings at My Meetings in Melbourne, Australia

he healings at the meetings were blessed. At every meeting I invited the sick to remain after the service, but in many of the meetings I prayed for all who would stand up and believe that the Lord would heal them. At other times I asked any who had pain to stand up, and I prayed for them from the platform.

At one meeting a lady stood saying she had pain in her head and was suffering from gallstones. When I prayed, the power of the Spirit came upon her.

A person in the hospital was healed of a tumor when a handkerchief was taken from me and laid on that person.

Mrs. Ingram tells of visiting a hospital and taking a handkerchief with her. Her friend was to be operated on the following Monday. On the Wednesday after that, when she visited her again, her friend told her that she had been on the operating table and the ether had been administered. When she regained consciousness, she discovered they had not operated because there was no need now for the operation. She was able to get up, and the swelling was all gone.

Mrs. A. Lavery of Collingwood writes, "I thank God for His blessed healing power. Hands were laid on my head. I had had blood pressure pains in my head for one year and six months, night and day. I know I am healed."

Mrs. Green of East Brunswick testifies, "I had mastoid trouble in my ear and general weakness throughout my body. Both of my kidneys had dropped an inch. I suffered terribly but had relief when prayed for. My ear began discharging. Now I am free."

Mr. R. Eddison of West Richmond was injured in a car accident. He had his ribs broken, collar bone broken, and lungs pierced. He was in the hospital for three weeks and suffered much pain for three months until prayed for in the meeting.

A woman who had been ill in bed for sixteen weeks was raised up by the Lord, was later baptized in water, and the following day received the baptism in the Holy Spirit.

A dying baby was healed.

A woman who had suffered pain in her legs for eleven years was set free.

Mrs. Rose Jesule writes, "The Lord touched my body in the audience, and I am free."

Another writes, "I have received the second handkerchief that you prayed over, and the Lord is blessing. This cancer is slowly drying up. I have had no more hemorrhages, and the terrible odor is leaving. Praise the Lord."

Sixteen

Abiding

*But I tell you truly, there are some standing
here who shall not taste death till they see
the kingdom of God.*
—Luke 9:27

ow God fascinates me with His Word. I read and read and read, and there is always something new. As I get deeper into the knowledge of the Bridegroom, I hear His voice saying, "The bride rejoices to hear the Bridegroom's voice." The Word is His voice, and the nearer we are to Jesus, the more we understand the principles of His mission. He came to take for Himself a people for His bride; He came to find those who would become the *"body of Christ"* (1 Cor. 12:27). God's message to us is that Jesus is going to take unto Himself a bride.

So, while we are here to talk about salvation, there are deeper truths God wants to show us. Not only is there salvation, but there is an eternal destiny awaiting us that is full of all the wonders God has in glory. God has given us this blessed revelation of how Jesus lived and loved and said these words: *"Some...shall not taste death till they see the kingdom of God* [come in power]" (Luke 9:27).

God's Glory Manifested in Christ

Jesus could pray until He was transfigured, until His face shone like the sun and His clothes became white and glistening (Matt. 17:2). Praise God, this same Jesus also said, *"I have power to lay* [My life] *down, and I have power to take it again"* (John 10:18). By wicked hands He was taken and crucified, but He was willing, for He had all power and could have called on legions of angels to deliver Him (Matt. 26:53). But His purpose was to save us and bring us into fellowship and oneness with Himself, so that the same life principles might be ours.

Jesus never looked back; He never withheld Himself. He went through death so that His life might be our portion in time and in eternity. He is the Lord Jesus Christ—the atonement for the whole world, the Son of God, the sinner's Friend. *"He was wounded for our transgressions"* (Isa. 53:5). He lived to manifest, to bring forth, the glory of God on earth. He gives His disciples the glory He had with the Father before the world began. He said, *"The glory which You gave Me I have given them"* (John 17:22).

So today, God *"will give grace and glory; no good thing will He withhold from those who walk uprightly"* (Ps. 84:11). He gives health, peace, joy in the Holy Spirit, and a life in Christ Jesus. It is wonderful, lovely. Shall we ever go back to Egypt? Shall we look back? Never!

Oh, you need not look for me down in Egypt's sand,
For I have pitched my tent far up in Beulah land.

There is redemption for all through the blood of Jesus. This redemption is heaven on earth; it is joy and peace in the Holy Spirit. It is a change from darkness to light, from the power of Satan to the power of God. It means to be made sons, heirs, and joint-heirs with Christ (Rom. 8:17).

Twice God rent the heavens with the words, *"This is My beloved Son, in whom I am well pleased"* (Matt. 3:17; 17:5). Yes, it is true that He was born in Bethlehem, that He worked as a carpenter, that He took upon Himself flesh. It is also true that God indwelt that flesh and manifested His glory, so that Christ was a perfect overcomer. He kept the law and fulfilled His commission, so that He could redeem us by laying down His life. Glory to God! Jesus was manifested in the flesh to destroy the power of the Devil (1 John 3:8). What does that mean? It means this: He is God's example to show us that what God did for and in Jesus, He can do for and in us.

Allow Christ to Change You

He can make us overcomers by dwelling in us by His mighty power and destroying the power of sin. He can transform us until we *"love righteousness and hate wickedness"* (Ps. 45:7), so that we can be holy.

We receive sonship because of His obedience. *"He learned obedience by the things which He suffered"* (Heb. 5:8). His family said He was beside Himself (Mark 3:21). The scribes said, *"He has a demon"*

(John 10:20) and *"'He has Beelzebub,' and, 'By the ruler of the demons He casts out demons'"* (Mark 3:22). They reviled Him and tried to kill Him by stoning Him, but He passed through the midst of the whole crowd. Then He saw a blind man and healed him as He was going through. (See John 8:59–9:7.)

Oh, He is lovely! Meditate on the beatitudes, the attributes, and the divine position Jesus manifested. This power of the new creation, this birth unto righteousness by faith in the Atonement, can transform and change you until you are controlled, dominated, and filled with the Spirit of Jesus. Though you are still in the body, you are governed by the Spirit, with *"fruit to holiness, and the end, everlasting life"* (Rom. 6:22). He was a firstfruits for us.

O Lord, reveal Yourself to this people, and give them genuine love and faith. Then they will withstand persecution, ridicule, and slander.

Christ loved you when you were yet a sinner, and He seeks your love in return. He imparts to you an in-wrought love by the Holy Spirit, changing you from faith to faith, from glory to glory.

What a Savior!

I am not surprised at Christ's face shining or at the presence of God appearing on the Mount (Matt. 17:2, 5). I am not surprised at anything that glorifies the Christ of God, who would lay down His own life to save the lost. Oh, what a Christ! When we were His enemies, He died for us (Rom. 5:8)!

Notice that Jesus had chances that were offered to no other human soul in the world. It was not only the glory of God that was offered to Him, but the manifestation of a human glory, for people in certain circles longed to make Him a king. Oh, if any of you heard that the whole country was longing to make you a king, you would lose your head and your senses and everything you have. But this blessed Christ of God retired and went to prayer. He was the greatest King that the world will ever know. He is the King of Kings and the Lord of Lords. *"Of His kingdom there will be no end"* (Luke 1:33). *"He shall see His seed, He shall prolong His days, and the pleasure of the LORD shall prosper in His hand"* (Isa. 53:10).

I wonder if there is any seed of the Lord Jesus in this place. Oh, you who believe you are the seed of the Son of God through promise, and the seed of the Son of God through faith, and the seed of the Son of God because His seed (the Word of God) is in you— all the seed in this place, let me see your hands. *"He shall see His seed, He shall prolong His days, and the pleasure of the LORD shall prosper in His hand."* Oh, hallelujah!

> *An Interpretation of Tongues:* "Glory to God, the living shall praise Him, for out of the dust of the earth He has brought forth a harvest of souls to praise Him for all eternity. He is seeing His seed, and the pleasure of the Lord is already prospering in His hand."

Yes, beloved, this is the day of the visitation of the Lord again in this place. Look at Him right now, you needy ones. As you gaze upon Him, you will be changed. A strength will come to you; you will exchange strength. He is the God of Jacob, the God of the helpless and the ruined.

The Devil had a big plan against Jacob, but there was one thing Jacob knew. He knew that God would fulfill His promise. At Bethel, God had let him see the ladder, where the angels began at the bottom and went to the top. Bethel was the place of prayer, the place of changing conditions, the place of the earthly entering the heavenly. God had promised him, and He brought him back to Bethel. But he was the same old Jacob, and as long as God allowed him to wrestle, he wrestled. That is a type of holding on to this world. Then God touched him. God has a way of touching us. Jacob cried, "Don't go until You have blessed me." (See Genesis 32:26.) God will bless you there. God will meet you at the place of helplessness and brokenness. Have you been there?

When Jesus was on the Mount in the glory, Moses and Elijah came to speak to Him about our salvation, about His death at Jerusalem. And when Jesus came down from the Mount of Transfiguration, He set His face forward to fulfill His commission for you and me. He went from the glory right to the cross. What a wonderful Jesus we have!

Don't Lose Your Deliverance

When Jesus came down among the crowd, a man cried out and said, "Help me, Lord; help me. Here is my son. The Devil takes him and tears him until he foams at the mouth, and there he lies prostrate. I brought him to Your disciples, but they could not help me." Oh, brothers and sisters, may God strengthen our hands and take away unbelief. Jesus said, *"O faithless generation...how long shall I bear with you? Bring him to Me"* (Mark 9:19). They brought him to Jesus, and Jesus cast out the evil spirit.

Did you know that even in the presence of Jesus these evil spirits tore the boy and left him as one dead? Just think about satanic power. The Devil goes about to kill, *"seeking whom he may devour"* (1 Pet. 5:8). May God save us and keep us in the place where the Devil has no power and no victory.

He has come; our Lord has come. Bless His name; has He come to you? He wants to come to you. He wants to be a sharer in your whole life. No, truly, He wants to transform your life through His power right now.

I pray to God that the demon powers that come out of everyone tonight will never get back in again. Oh, if I could only show you what it means to be de-livered by the power of Jesus, and what it means (now hear what I say) to lose your deliverance through your own folly.

There was a case like this. A man possessed with demon power and sickness and every weakness came to Jesus. Jesus cast the evil spirit out, and the man was made whole. But then, instead of the man seeking the Holy Spirit and the light of God and walking as blind Bartimaeus walked with Jesus when he was healed—instead of that, he went back into sin as soon as he could. God save us. The evil spirit had nowhere to go, and it went to the Savior to see if it could gain an entrance. Then it went back and found that, al-though it appeared that this man's life was swept clean and in order, the man had no inhabitant in him. He did not have Christ and the power of the Spirit. So the evil spirits entered into that man, and his case was worse than before. (See Matthew 12:43–45.)

If you people want healing by the power of God, it means your lives have to be filled with God. Will it last? Get Jesus on board, and it will last forever. You cannot keep yourself. No man is capable of standing against the schemes of the Devil by himself. But when you get Jesus in you, you are equal to a million devils. Not only must our lives be swept clean and put in order, but we must see that the power of God comes to inhabit us. No one is safe without Christ, but the weak man is capable if he is in Christ Jesus. Are you willing to surrender yourself to God tonight so that Satan will have no dominion over you? In the name of Jesus, I ask you.

The power of God is just the same today,
    It does not matter what the people say.
Whatever God has promised He is able to perform,
    For the power of God is just the same today.

Seventeen

Common Sense

 have had people ask me, "Is it every Christian's privilege to have his eyes preserved so that he never needs to wear glasses?" That is the question I will answer here.

The aging process affects every person. There are many people who have been praying ever since they were ten years old, and if praying and the life within them could have altered the situation, it would have been altered. But I see that many are here today with gray hair and white hair; this shows that the natural man decays, and you cannot do what you like with it. But the supernatural man may so abound in the natural man that it never decays; it can be replaced by divine life.

There comes a time in life when at age fifty or so, all eyes, without exception, begin to grow dim. However, although the natural man has had a change, I believe and affirm that the supernatural power can be so ministered to us that even our eyesight can be preserved right through. But I say this: any person who professes to have faith and then gets a large print Bible so that he will not need glasses is a fool. It presents a false impression before the people. He must see that if he wants to carry a Bible that is not huge, his eyesight may require some help, or he may not be able to read correctly.

I have been preaching faith to my people for thirty years. When my daughter came back from Africa and saw her mother and me with glasses, she was amazed. When our people saw us put glasses on the first time, they were very troubled. They were no more troubled than we were. But I found it was far better to be honest with the people and acknowledge my condition than get a Bible with large print and deceive the people and say that my eyesight was all right. I like to be honest.

My eyesight gave way at about age fifty-three, and somehow God is doing something. I am now sixty-eight, and I do not need a stronger prescription than I needed then, and I am satisfied that God is restoring me.

When I was seeking this way of divine healing, I was baffled because all the people who had mighty testimonies of divine healing were wearing glasses. I said, "I cannot go on with this thing. I am baffled every time I see the people preaching divine healing wearing glasses." And I got such a bitterness in my spirit that God had to settle me along that line—and I believe that I have not yet fully paid the price.

My eyes will be restored, but until then, I will not deceive anybody. I will wear glasses until I can see perfectly.

A woman came up to me one day, and I noticed that she had no teeth. "Why," I said, "your mouth is very uneven. Your gums have dropped in some places, and they are very uneven."

"Yes," she said, "I am trusting the Lord for a new set of teeth."

"That is very good," I said. "How long have you been trusting Him for them?"

"Three years."

"Look here," I said, "I would be like Gideon. I would put the fleece out, and I would tell the Lord that I would trust Him to send me teeth in ten days or money to buy a set in ten days. Whichever came first, I would believe it was from Him."

In eight days, fifty dollars came to her from a person whom she had never been acquainted with in any way, and it bought her a beautiful set of teeth— and she looked nice in them.

Often I pray for a person's eyesight, and as soon as he is prayed for, he believes, and God stimulates his faith, but his eyesight is about the same. "What should I do?" he asks. "Should I go away without my glasses?"

"Can you see perfectly?" I ask. "Do you need any help?"

"Yes. If I were to go without my glasses, I would stumble."

"Put your glasses on," I say, "for when your faith is perfected, you will no longer need your glasses. When God perfects your faith, your glasses will drop off. But as long as you need them, use them."

You can take that for what you like, but I believe in common sense.

Eighteen

Divine Life Brings
Divine Health

ee from Mark 1 how Jesus was quickened by the power of the Spirit of God and how He was driven by the Spirit into the wilderness (vv. 9–12). See how John also was so filled with the Spirit of God that he had a "cry" within him, and the cry moved all Israel (vv. 2–5). When God gets hold of a man in the Spirit, he can have a new cry—something in God's order. A man may cry for fifty years without the Spirit of the Lord, and the more he cries, the less people notice him. But if he is filled with the Holy Spirit and cries once, people feel the effects.

Energized by the Spirit

So there is a necessity for every one of us to be filled with God. It is not sufficient to have just a touch or to be filled with just a desire. Only one thing will meet the needs of the people, and that is for you to be immersed in the life of God. This means that God takes you and fills you with His Spirit until you live right in God. He does this so that *"whether you eat or drink, or whatever you do,* [it may be] *all to the glory of God"* (1 Cor. 10:31). In that place you will find that all your strength and all your mind and all your soul are filled with a zeal, not only for worship, but for proclamation. This proclamation is accompanied by all the power of God, which must move satanic power and disturb the world.

The reason the world is not seeing Jesus is that Christian people are not filled with Jesus. They are satisfied with attending meetings weekly, reading the Bible occasionally, and praying sometimes. Beloved, if God lays hold of you by the Spirit, you will find that there is an end of everything and a beginning of God. Your whole body will become seasoned with a divine likeness of God. Not only will He have begun to use you, but He will have taken you in hand, so that you might be *"a vessel for honor"* (2 Tim. 2:21). Our lives are not to be for ourselves, for if we live for ourselves we will die (Rom. 8:13); but if *"by the Spirit* [we] *put to death the deeds of the body,* [we] *will live"* (v. 13). He who lives in the Spirit is subject to the powers of God, but he who lives for himself will die. The man who lives in the Spirit lives a life of freedom and joy and blessing and service—a life that brings blessing to others. God would have us see that we must live in the Spirit.

You Can Be like Jesus

In Mark 1, we have two important factors in the Spirit. One is Jesus filled with the Holy Spirit and driven by the Spirit's power. The other is John the Baptist, who was so filled with the Spirit of God that his one aim was to go out preaching. We find him in the wilderness. What a strange place to be! Beloved, it was quite natural for Jesus, after He had served a whole day among the multitudes, to want to go to His Father and pray all night. Why? He wanted a source of strength and power; He wanted an association with His Father that would bring everything else to a place of submission.

After Jesus had been on the mountain communing with His Father and after He had been clothed with God's holy presence and Spirit, when He met the demon power, it had to go. (See Matthew 17:1–9, 14–18.) When He met sickness, it had to leave. He came from the mountain with power to meet whatever needs the people had.

I do not know what your state of grace is— whether you are saved or not—but it is an awful thing for me to see people who profess to be Christians lifeless, powerless, and in a place where their lives are so parallel to unbelievers' lives that it is difficult to tell which place they are in, whether in the flesh or in the Spirit. Many people live in the place that is described to us by Paul in Romans 7:25: *"With the mind I myself serve the law of God, but with the flesh the law of sin."* That is the place where sin is in the ascendancy. But when the power of God comes to you, it is to separate you from yourself. It is destruction of yourself, annihilation. It is to move you from nature to grace, making you mighty over the powers of the Enemy and making you know that you have now begun to live a life of faith in the Son of God.

Turning Struggles into Rest

I pray that God will give us a way out of difficulties and into rest. The writer to the Hebrews told us that *"there remains therefore a rest for the people of God"* (Heb. 4:9). Those who have entered into that rest have ceased from their own works (v. 10). Oh, what a blessed state of rest that is, to cease from your own works. There God is enthroned in your life, and you are working for Him by a new order. If you preach, you no longer struggle to preach in the old way of sermonettes. God wants to bring you forth as a flame of fire with a message from God, with a truth that will disturb the powers of Satan, and with an unlimited supply for every needy soul. Then, just as John moved all of Israel with a cry, you, by the power of the Holy Spirit, will move the people.

This is what Jesus meant when He said to Nicodemus,

> *Unless one is born again, he cannot see the kingdom of God....*[For] *that which is born of the flesh is flesh, and that which is born of the Spirit is spirit. Do not marvel that I said to you, "You must be born again."*
>
> *(John 3:3, 6–7)*

Oh, if you only knew what those words mean. To be born of God! It means no less than God being born anew in us—a new order of God; a new plan; a new faith by God; a new child of God; a new life from God; a new creation living in the world but not of the world, reigning in life over all the powers of the world, over whom *"sin shall not have dominion"* (Rom. 6:14).

Life by the Spirit

How will we reach these beatitudes in the Spirit? How will we come into the presence of God? How will we attain to these divine principles? Beloved, it is not in the flesh and never was! How can it be, when the Scripture plainly says that if we live according to the flesh we will die (Rom. 8:13)? But if we live *"by the Spirit,"* we will *"put to death the deeds of the body"* (v. 13) and will find that *"mortality* [will] *be swallowed up by life"* (2 Cor. 5:4). Life will prevail in the body and in the mind, over self, over disease, over everything in the world, so that we may walk around without being distracted by any bodily ailments. Are we in this place?

I dare say that many of you are in a bound condition, with lots of things to remind you that you have a body. Do you not know that Jesus Christ was manifested to *"destroy the works of the devil"* (1 John 3:8), to loose you from the bondage of self, and to free you from the bondage of the present evil world? Do you not know that Jesus came for the express purpose of destroying the flesh?

Jesus proceeded from the Father and went to the Father. That blessed, blessed Jesus. Have you received Him? I have no doubt that if I were to ask you whether you believe in Jesus, many of you would say that you have believed in Jesus all your lives. But if I were to ask, "Are you saved?" many of you would unhesitatingly reply that you have never done anything wrong in your whole lives but have always

done what is right and honorable. Oh, you hypo-
crites! You self-righteous vipers! There is no such
person on the earth. *"All have sinned and fall short
of the glory of God"* (Rom. 3:23, emphasis added).
How will we get rid of our sins? *"The blood of Jesus
Christ His Son cleanses us from all sin"* (1 John 1:7).
How will we get rid of our diseases? *"The blood of
Jesus Christ His Son cleanses us from all* [diseases]."
You cannot think about that blessed One without
becoming holy.

We have a Scripture that says, *"Whatever is
born of God overcomes the world....Who is he who
overcomes the world, but he who believes that Jesus
is the Son of God?"* (1 John 5:4–5). The one who is
born again overcomes the world, and if you find that
the world overcomes you, you can be sure that you
have never known this Jesus. Jesus *"was manifested...*[to] *destroy the works of the devil"* (1 John
3:8).

I want to talk until you are shaken and disturbed, until you see where you are. If I can get you
to search the Scriptures after I leave this place and
to see if I have been preaching according to the Word
of God, then I will be pleased. Wake up to see that
the Scriptures have life and freedom for you. They
have nothing less than power to make you sons of
God, free in the Holy Spirit.

Now Jesus came to bring back to us what was
forfeited in the Garden. Adam and Eve were there—
free from sin and disease—and first sin came, then
disease, and then death. People want to say this is
not so! But I tell you, "Get the Devil out of you, and
you will have a different body. Get disease out, and
you will get the Devil out."

Jesus rebuked sickness, and it went. So this morning, I want to bring you to a place where you will see that you are healed. You must give God your life. You must see that sickness has to go and that God has to come in. You must see that your life has to be clean and that God will keep you holy. You must see that you have to walk before God and that He will make you perfect, for God says, *"Pursue...holiness, without which no one will see the Lord"* (Heb. 12:14). Moreover, as *"we walk in the light as He is in the light, we have fellowship with one another, and the blood of Jesus Christ His Son cleanses us from all sin"* (1 John 1:7).

A Place of Victory

I want to say to you believers that there is a very blessed place for you to attain to, and the place where God wants you is a place of victory. When the Spirit of the Lord comes into your life, there must be victory. The disciples, before they received the Holy Spirit, were always in bondage. Jesus said to them one day, just before the Crucifixion, *"One of you will betray Me"* (Matt. 26:21), and they were so conscious of their inability, helplessness, and human depravity that they said to Jesus, *"Is it I?"* (v. 22). Then Peter was ashamed that he had taken that stand, and he rose up and said, *"Even if all are made to stumble because of You, I will never be made to stumble"* (v. 33). Likewise, the others rose up and declared that neither would they (v. 35), but every one of them did leave Him.

However, beloved, after they received the power of the outpouring of the Holy Spirit, they were made as bold as lions to meet any difficulty. They were made to stand any test. When the power of God fell upon them in the Upper Room, these same men who had failed before the Crucifixion came out in front of all those people who were gathered together and accused them of crucifying the Lord of Glory. They were bold. What had made them like this? Purity. I tell you, purity is bold. Take, for instance, a little child. He will gaze straight into your eyes for as long as you like, without looking away once. The purer a person is, the bolder he is. I tell you, God wants to bring us into that divine purity of heart and life, that holy boldness. Not arrogance, not big-headedness, not self-righteousness, but a pure, holy, divine appointment by One who will come in and live with you. He will defy the powers of Satan and put you in a place of victory, a place of overcoming the world.

You never inherited that kind of victory from the flesh. That is a gift from God, by the Spirit, to all who obey. Therefore, no one can say he wishes he were an overcomer but that he has failed and failed until he has no hope. Beloved, God can make *you* an overcomer. When the Spirit of God comes into your body, He transforms you; He gives you life. Oh, there is a life in the Spirit that makes you *"free from the law of sin and death"* (Rom. 8:2) and gives you boldness and personality. It is the personality of the Deity. It is God in you.

I tell you that God is able to so transform you and bring you into order by the Spirit that you can become a new creation after God's order. There is no such thing as defeat for the believer. Without the Cross, without Christ's righteousness, without the new birth, without the indwelling Christ, without this divine incoming of God, I see myself as a failure. But God the Holy Spirit can come in and take our place until we are renewed in righteousness, until we are made the children of God.

Do you think that God made you in order to watch you fail? God never made men in order to see them fail. He made men in order that they might be sons who walk the earth in power. So when I look at you, I know that God can give you the capability to bring everything into subjection. Yes, you can have the power of Christ dwelling in you. His power can bring every evil thing under your feet and make you master over the flesh and the Devil. His power can work until nothing rises within you except what will magnify and glorify the Lord.

God wants me to show you Jesus' disciples, who were very frail like you and me, so that we, too, may now be filled with God and become ambassadors of this wonderful truth I am preaching. We see Peter, frail, helpless, and at every turn a failure. However, God filled that man with the Spirit of His righteousness until he went up and down as bold as a lion. Moreover, when he faced death—even crucifixion—he counted himself unworthy of being crucified like his Lord and asked that his murderers would put him upside down on the cross. He had a deep submissiveness and a power that was greater than all flesh. Peter had received the power of God.

God's Unfailing Word

The Scriptures do not tell two different stories. They tell the truth. I want you to know the truth, *"and the truth shall make you free"* (John 8:32).

What is truth? Jesus said, *"I am the way, the truth, and the life"* (John 14:6). He also said, *"He who believes in Me, as the Scripture has said, out of his heart will flow rivers of living water"* (John 7:38). He said this concerning the Spirit, who would be given after Jesus had been glorified (v. 39).

I find nothing in the Bible but holiness, and nothing in the world but worldliness. Therefore, if I live in the world, I will become worldly; on the other hand, if I live in the Bible, I will become holy. This is the truth, *"and the truth shall make you free"* (John 8:32).

God's Transforming Power

The power of God can remodel you. He can make you hate sin and love righteousness (Ps. 45:7). He can take away bitterness and hatred and covetousness and malice. He can so consecrate you by His power, through His blood, that you are made pure and every bit holy—pure in mind, heart, and actions, pure right through.

God has given me the way of life, and I want to faithfully give it to you, as though this were the last day I had to live. Jesus is the best blessing, and you can take Him away with you this morning. God gave His Son to be *"the propitiation for* [y]*our sins, and not for* [y]*ours only but also for the whole world"* (1 John 2:2).

Jesus came to make us free from sin—free from disease and pain. When I see a person diseased and in pain, I have great compassion on him. When I lay my hands upon him, I know God intends for men to be so filled with Him that the power of sin has no effect on them. He intends for them to go forth, as I am doing, to help the needy, sick, and afflicted. But what is the main thing? To preach *"the kingdom of God and His righteousness"* (Matt. 6:33). Jesus came to do this. John also came preaching repentance (Mark 1:4). The disciples began by preaching *"repentance toward God and faith toward our Lord Jesus Christ"* (Acts 20:21). I tell you, beloved, if you have really been changed by God, there is a repentance in your heart that you will never regret having there.

Through the revelation of the Word of God, we find that divine healing is solely for the glory of God. Moreover, salvation is to make you know that now you have to be inhabited by another, even God, and that now you have to walk with God *"in newness of life"* (Rom. 6:4).

Nineteen

The Grace of Long-Suffering and the Gifts of Healings

To another [is given] *faith by the same Spirit, to another gifts of healings by the same Spirit.*
—1 Corinthians 12:9

his morning we will move on to the gifts of healings. However, you cannot expect to understand the gifts and to understand the Epistles unless you have the Holy Spirit. All the Epistles are written to a baptized people, not to the unregenerate. They are written to those who have grown to maturity and now manifest the characteristics of the Christ of God. Do not jump into the Epistles before you have come in at the gate of the baptism in the Spirit.

I believe that this teaching that God is helping me bring to you will make you thoroughly restless and discontented until God is done dealing with you. If we want to know the mind of God through the Epistles, nothing will unveil the truth except the revelation of the Spirit Himself. He gives the utterance; He opens the door. Don't live in a state of poverty when we are surrounded by the rarest gems of the latest word from God. As Matthew 7:7–8 says,

> *Ask, and it will be given to you; seek, and you will find; knock, and it will be opened to you. For everyone who asks receives, and he who seeks finds, and to him who knocks it will be opened.*

These verses are backed by the authority of God's Word. Remember, the authority of God's Word is Jesus. These are the utterances by Jesus' Spirit to us this morning.

Higher Heights

I come to you with a great inward desire to wake you up to your great possibilities. Your responsibilities will be great, but not as great as your possibilities. You will always find that God's supply is more than abundant, and He wants you to agree with His way of thinking so that you are not restricted by yourself. Be enlarged in God!

> *An Interpretation of Tongues:* "It is that which God has chosen for us, which is mightier than we. It is that which is bottomless, higher than the heights, more lovely than all beside. And God in a measure presses you out to believe all things so that you may 'endure all things' and 'lay hold on eternal life' through the power of the Spirit."

How to Minister the Gifts of Healings

The gifts of healings are wonderful gifts. There is a difference between having a gift of healing and *"gifts of healings"* (1 Cor. 12:9). God wants us not to come short in anything (1 Cor. 1:7).

I like this term *"gifts of healings."* To have these gifts, I must bring myself into conformity with the mind and will of God. It would be impossible for you to have gifts of healings unless you possessed that blessed fruit of long-suffering. You will find that these gifts run parallel to that which will bring them into operation.

How is it possible to minister the gifts of healings considering the peculiarities there are in the churches and the many evil powers of Satan that confront us and possess bodies? The person who wants to go through with God and exercise the gifts of healings has to be a person of long-suffering, always having a word of comfort. If the one who is in distress and helpless doesn't see eye to eye with us about every matter and doesn't get all he wants, long-suffering will bear and forbear. Long-suffering is a grace Jesus lived in and moved in. He was filled with compassion, and God will never be able to move us to help the needy until we reach that place.

You might think by the way I went about praying for the sick that I was sometimes unloving and rough, but oh, friends, you have no idea what I see behind the sickness and the one who is afflicted. I am not dealing with the person; I am dealing with the satanic forces that are binding the afflicted. As far as people go, my heart is full of love and compassion for all, but I fail to see how you will ever reach a place where God will be able to use you until you get angry at the Devil.

One day a pet dog followed a lady out of her house and ran all around her feet. She said to the dog, "I cannot have you with me today." The dog wagged its tail and made a great fuss. "Go home, pet," she said, but it didn't go. At last she shouted roughly, "Go home!" and off it went.

Some people play with the Devil like that. "Poor thing!" they say. The Devil can stand all the comfort anybody in the world could give him. Cast him out! You are not dealing with the person; you are dealing with the Devil. If you say with authority, "Come out, you demons, in the name of the Lord!" they must come out. You will always be right when you dare to treat sickness as the Devil's work.

Gifts of healings are so varied that you will often find the gift of discernment operating in connection with them. Moreover, the manifestations of the Spirit are given to us *"for the profit of all"* (1 Cor. 12:7).

You must never treat a cancer case as anything else but a living evil spirit that is destroying the body. It is one of the worst kind of evil spirits I know. Not that the Devil has anything good—every disease of the Devil is bad, either to a greater or lesser degree—but this form of disease is one that you must cast out.

Miracles of Healing

Among the first people I met in Victoria Hall was a woman who had breast cancer. As soon as the cancer was cursed, it died and stopped bleeding. The next thing that happened was that her body cast it out, because the natural body has no room for dead matter. When it came out, it was like a big ball with thousands of fibers. All these fibers had spread out into the flesh, but the moment the evil power was destroyed, they had no power.

Jesus gave us power to bind and power to loose (Matt. 16:19); we must bind the evil powers and loose the afflicted and set them free. There are many cases where Satan has control of the mind, and not all those under satanic influence are in asylums.

I will tell you what freedom is. No one who enjoys the fullness of the Spirit and a clear knowledge of redemption should notice that he has a body. You ought to be able to sleep, eat, and digest your food and not be conscious of your body. You should be a living epistle of God's thought and mind, walking up and down in the world without pain. That is redemption. To be fully in the will of God, to fully possess the perfection of redemption, we should not have pain of any kind.

I have had some experience along these lines. When I was weak and helpless and friends were expecting me to die, it was in that distressing place that I saw the fullness of redemption. I read and reread the Ninety-first Psalm and claimed long life. *"With long life I will satisfy him"*—and what else?— *"and show him My salvation"* (Ps. 91:16). His salvation is greater than long life. The salvation of God is deliverance from everything, and here I am. At least twenty-five or thirty people were expecting me to die; now at sixty-three I feel young. So there is something more in this truth that I am preaching than mere words. God has not designed us for anything else than to be firstfruits (James 1:18), sons of God with power over all the power of the Enemy, living in the world but not of it. (See John 17:14–16.)

Dealing with Demons

In casting out demons, we have to be careful about who gives the command. Man may say, "Come out," but unless his command is by the Spirit of God, his words are useless.

In the past, during the middle of the night, the Devil would have a good time with me and would try to give me a bad time. I had a real conflict with evil powers, and the only deliverance I got was when I bound them in the name of the Lord.

I remember one day walking with a man who was demon-possessed. We were going through a thickly crowded place, and this man became loud and unruly. I boldly faced him, and the demons came out of him. However, I wasn't careful, and these demons fastened themselves on me right on the street so that I couldn't move.

Sometimes when I am ministering on the platform and the powers of the Devil attack me, the people think I am casting demons out of them, but I am casting them out of myself. The people couldn't understand the situation when I cast those evil spirits out of that man on the street, but I understood. The man who had that difficulty is now preaching and is one of the finest men we have. But the requirement for his deliverance was that someone *"bind the strong man"* (Matt. 12:29 KJV).

You must be sure of your ground; you must be sure that there is a power mightier than you that is destroying the Devil. Take your position from the first epistle of John and say, *"Greater is he that is in [me], than he that is in the world"* (1 John 4:4 KJV). If you think the power comes from you, you make a great mistake. It comes from your being filled with Him, from His acting in the place of you—your thoughts, your words, your all being used by the Spirit of God.

Miracles in Norway

In Norway we had a place seating 1,500 people. When I arrived, it was packed, and hundreds were unable to get in. Some policemen were standing there, and I thought that the first thing I would do would be to preach to the people outside and then go in. I addressed the policemen and said, "You see this condition. I have come with a message to help everybody, and it hurts me very much to find as many people outside as in. I want the promise of you police officials that you will give us the marketplace tomorrow. Will you do it?" They put up their hands to show that they would.

The next day was a beautiful April day, and there was a big stand about ten feet high in the great park, where thousands of people gathered. After the preaching, we had some wonderful cases of healing. One man came one hundred miles, bringing his food with him. Nothing had passed through his stomach for over a month, for there was a great cancerous growth there. He was healed in the meeting and, opening up his lunch, began eating before all the people.

Then there was a young woman who came with a stiff hand. When I cursed the spirit of infirmity, it was instantly cast out, and the arm was free. She waved it over her head and said, "My father is the chief of police." She also said, "I have been bound since I was a girl."

At the close of the meeting, Satan afflicted two people with fits. That was my day! I jumped down to where they were and in the name of Jesus delivered them. People said, "Oh, isn't he rough!" but when they saw those afflicted stand up and praise God, that was a time of rejoicing.

The Price of Miracles

Oh, we must wake up, stretch our faith, and believe God! Before God could bring me to this place, He had to break me a thousand times. I have wept, I have groaned, I have travailed night after night until God broke me. Until God has mowed you down, you will never have this long-suffering for others.

When I was at Cardiff, the Lord healed a woman right in the meeting. She was afflicted with ulcers, and while we were singing, she fell full length and cried in such a way that I felt something must be done. I knelt down alongside of the woman and laid my hands on her body. Instantly the powers of the Devil were destroyed. She was delivered from ulcers, rose up, and joined in the singing.

We have been seeing wonderful miracles in these last days, and they are only a little of what we are going to see. When I say "going to see," I do not want to imply ten years from now, or even two years.

I believe we are right on the threshold of wonderful things.

You must not think that these gifts fall on you like ripe cherries. You pay a price for everything you get from God. There is nothing worth having that you do not have to pay for, either temporally or spiritually.

Ministering to a Lame Man

I remember when I was at Antwerp and Brussels. The power of God was very mighty upon me there. Going on to London, I called on some friends. To show you the leading of the Lord, these friends said, "Oh, God sent you here. How much we need you!" They sent a wire to a place where there was a young man twenty-six years old who had been in bed eighteen years. His body was much bigger than an ordinary body because of inactivity, and his legs were like a child's; instead of bone, there was cartilage. He had never been able to dress himself.

When his family got the wire, the father dressed him, and he was sitting in a chair. I felt it was one of the opportunities of my life. I said to this young man, "What is the greatest desire of your heart?" "Oh," he said, "to be filled with the Holy Spirit!" I put my hands upon him and said, "Receive; receive the Holy Spirit." Instantly he became drunk with the Spirit and fell off the chair like a big bag of potatoes. I saw what God could do with a helpless cripple. First, his head began shaking terrifically; then his back began moving very fast, and then his legs. Then he spoke clearly in tongues, and we wept and praised the Lord. Looking at his legs, I saw that they were still as they had been, by all appearances, and this is where I missed it.

These "missings" are sometimes God's opportunities of teaching us important lessons. He will teach us through our weaknesses what is not faith. It was not faith for me to look at that body, but human nature. The man who wants to work the works of God must never look at conditions but at Jesus, in whom everything is complete.

I looked at the boy, and there was absolutely no help. I turned to the Lord and said, "Lord, tell me what to do," and He did. He said, "Command him to walk in My name." This is where I missed it. I looked at his conditions, and I got the father to help lift him up to see if his legs had strength. We did our best, but he and I together could not move him. Then the Lord showed me my mistake, and I said, "God, forgive me." I got right down and repented and said to the Lord, "Please tell me again." God is so good. He never leaves us to ourselves. Again He said to me, "Command him in My name to walk." So I shouted, "Arise and walk in the name of Jesus." Did he do it? No, I declare he never walked. He was lifted up by the power of God in a moment, and he ran. The door was wide open; he ran out across the road into a field where he ran up and down and came back. Oh, it was a miracle!

Can God Use You?

There are miracles to be performed, and these miracles will be accomplished by us when we understand the perfect plan of His spiritual graces that has come down to us. These things will come to us when we come to a place of brokenness, of surrender, of wholehearted yieldedness, where we decrease but God increases (John 3:30), and where we dwell and live in Him.

Will you allow Him to be the choice of your thoughts? Submit to Him, the God of all grace, so that you may be well furnished with faith for every good work, so that the mind of the Lord may have free course in you, so that it may run and be glorified (2 Thess. 3:1). Submit so that the heathen will know the truth, so that the uttermost parts of the earth will be filled with the glory of the Lord as the waters cover the deep (Isa. 11:9).

Twenty

I Am the Lord
Who Heals You

Is anyone among you sick? Let him call for the
elders of the church, and let them pray over him,
anointing him with oil in the name of the Lord.
And the prayer of faith will save the sick, and
the Lord will raise him up. And if he has
committed sins, he will be forgiven.
—James 5:14–15

e have in this precious Word a real basis for
the truth of healing. In these verses God
gives very definite instructions to the sick.
If you are sick, your part is to call for the
elders of the church; it is their part to anoint and
pray for you in faith. Then the whole situation rests
with the Lord. When you have been anointed and
prayed for, you can rest assured that the Lord will
raise you up. It is the Word of God.

I believe that we all can see that the church
cannot play with this business. If believers turn
away from these clear instructions, they are in a

place of tremendous danger. Those who refuse to obey do so to their unspeakable loss.

In connection with this, James told us,

> *If anyone among you wanders from the truth, and someone turns him back, let him know that he who turns a sinner from the error of his way will save a soul from death and cover a multitude of sins.*　　*(James 5:19–20)*

Many turn away from the Lord like King Asa, who *"in his disease...did not seek the LORD, but the physicians"* (2 Chron. 16:12). Consequently, *"he died"* (v. 13). I take it that this passage in James means that if one induces another to turn back to the Lord, he will save that person from death, and God will forgive that person of a multitude of sins. This Scripture can also largely apply to salvation. If you turn away from any part of God's truth, the Enemy will certainly get an advantage over you.

Does the Lord meet those who look to Him for healing and who obey the instructions set forth in the book of James? Most assuredly. He will undertake for the most extreme case.

Only last night a woman came into the meeting suffering terribly. Her whole arm was filled with poison, and her blood was so poisoned that it was certain to bring her to her death. We rebuked the thing, and she was here this morning and told us that she was without pain and had slept all night, a thing she had not done for two months. To God be all the praise! You will find that He will do this kind of thing all along.

God provides the double cure, for even if sin has been the cause of the sickness, His Word declares in James 5:15, *"If he has committed sins, he will be forgiven."*

Faith in Jesus and Submission to Others

You ask, "What is faith?" Faith is the principle of the Word of God. The Holy Spirit, who inspired the Word, is called the Spirit of Truth. As we *"receive with meekness the implanted word"* (James 1:21), faith springs up in our hearts—faith in the sacrifice of Calvary; faith in the shed blood of Jesus; faith in the fact that He took our weaknesses, bore our sicknesses, carried our pains, and is our life today.

God has chosen us to help one another. We dare not be independent. He brings us to a place where we submit ourselves to one another. If we refuse to do this, we get away from the Word of God and out of the place of faith. I have been in this place once, and I trust I will never be there again. It happened one time when I went to a meeting. I was very, very sick, and I got worse and worse. I knew the perfect will of God was for me to humble myself and ask the elders to pray for me. I put it off, and the meeting ended. I went home without being anointed and prayed for, and everyone in the house caught the thing I was suffering with.

My boys did not know anything else but to trust the Lord as the family Physician, and my youngest boy, George, cried down from the attic, "Dadda, come." I cried, "I cannot come. The whole thing is from me. I will have to repent and ask the Lord to forgive me." I made up my mind to humble myself before the whole church. Then I rushed to the attic and laid my hands on my boy in the name of Jesus. I placed my hands on his head, and the pain left and went lower; he cried, "Put your hands lower." This continued until at last the pain went right down to his feet, and as I placed my hands on his feet, he was completely delivered. Some evil power had evidently gotten hold of him, and as I laid my hands on the different parts of the body, it left. (We have to see the difference between anointing the sick and casting out demons.) God will always be gracious when we humble ourselves before Him and come to a place of brokenness of spirit.

Praying for a Paralytic

I was in Le Havre, France, and the power of God was being mightily manifested. A Greek named Felix attended the meeting and became very zealous for God. He was very eager to get all the Catholics he could to the meeting in order that they could see that God was graciously visiting France. He found a certain bedridden woman who was fixed in a certain position and could not move, and he told her about the Lord's healing at the meetings and said that he would get me to come if she wished. She said, "My husband is a Catholic, and he would never allow anyone who is not a Catholic to see me."

She asked her husband to allow me to come and told him what Felix had told her about the power of God working in our midst. He said, "I will have no Protestant enter my house." She said, "You know that the doctors cannot help me, and the priests cannot help. Won't you let this man of God pray for me?" He finally consented, and I went to the house. The simplicity of this woman and her childlike faith were beautiful to see.

I showed her my oil bottle and said to her, "Here is oil. It is a symbol of the Holy Spirit. When that comes upon you, the Holy Spirit will begin to work, and the Lord will raise you up." God did something the moment the oil fell upon her. I looked toward the window, and I saw Jesus. (I have seen Him often. There is no painting that is a bit like Him; no artist can ever depict the beauty of my lovely Lord.) The woman felt the power of God in her body and cried, "I'm free! My hands are free, my shoulders are free, and oh, I see Jesus! I'm free! I'm free!"

The vision vanished, and the woman sat up in bed. Her legs were still bound, and I said to her, "I'll put my hands on your legs, and you will be free entirely." As I put my hands on those legs covered with bedclothes, I looked and saw the Lord again. She saw Him, too, and cried, "He's there again. I'm free! I'm free!" She rose from her bed and walked around the room praising God, and we were all in tears as we saw His wonderful works. As we are told in James 5:15, *"the Lord will raise* [them] *up"* when the conditions are met.

Our Wonderful Lord

We have a big God. We have a wonderful Jesus. We have a glorious Comforter. God's canopy is over you and will cover you at all times, preserving you from evil. *"Under His wings you shall take refuge"* (Ps. 91:4). *"The word of God is living and powerful"*

(Heb. 4:12), and in its treasures you will find eternal life. If you dare trust this wonderful Lord, this Lord of Life, you will find in Him everything you need.

So many are trying drugs, quacks, pills, and plasters. You will find that if you dare trust God, He will never fail. *"The prayer of faith will save the sick, and the Lord will raise him up"* (James 5:15). Do you trust Him? He is worthy to be trusted.

Delivering a Maniac

One time I was asked to go to Weston-super-Mare, a seaside resort in the western part of England. I learned from a telegram that a man had lost his reason and had become a raving maniac, and some people there wanted me to come and pray for him. I arrived at the place, and the wife said to me, "Will you stay with my husband?" I agreed, and in the middle of the night, an evil power laid hold of him. It was awful. I put my hand on his head, and his hair was like toothpicks standing on end. God gave deliverance—a temporary deliverance. At six o'clock the next morning, I felt that it was necessary that I get out of that house for a short time.

The man saw me going and cried out, "If you leave me, there is no hope." But I felt that I had to go. As I left, I saw a woman with a Salvation Army bonnet on, and I knew that she was going to their seven o'clock prayer meeting. I said to the captain who was in charge of the meeting, when I saw he was about to sing a hymn, "Captain, don't sing. Let's go to prayer." He agreed, and I prayed my heart out. Then I grabbed my hat and rushed out of the hall.

They all thought they had had a madman in their prayer meeting that morning.

I went down the road, and there was the man I had spent the night with, rushing down toward the sea without a particle of clothing on, about to drown himself. I cried, "In the name of Jesus, come out of him." The man fell full length on the ground, and that evil power went out of him never to return. His wife came rushing after him, and the husband was restored to her in a perfect mental condition.

Being Kept by God's Power

There are evil powers, but Jesus is greater than all evil powers. There are tremendous diseases, but Jesus is the Healer. There is no case too hard for Him. The Lion of Judah will break every chain. He came to relieve the oppressed and to set the captive free (Luke 4:18). He came to bring redemption, to make us as perfect as man was before the Fall.

People want to know how to be kept by the power of God. Every position of grace into which you are led—forgiveness, healing, any kind of deliverance—will be contested by Satan. He will contend for your body. When you are saved, Satan will come around and say, "See, you are not saved." The Devil is a liar.

I remember the story of the man whose life was swept and put in order. The evil power had been swept out of him. But the man remained in a stationary position. If the Lord heals you, you dare not remain in a stationary position. The evil spirit came back to that man, found his house swept, and took seven others worse than himself and dwelt there.

The last stage of that man was worse than the first. (See Matthew 12:43–45.) Be sure to get filled with God. Get an Occupier. Be filled with the Spirit.

God has a million ways of undertaking for those who go to Him for help. He has deliverance for every captive. He loves you so much that He even says, *"Before they call, I will answer"* (Isa. 65:24). Don't turn Him away.

Twenty-One

What It Means to Be Full of the Holy Spirit

Now in those days, when the number of the disciples was multiplying, there arose a complaint against the Hebrews by the Hellenists, because their widows were neglected in the daily distribution. Then the twelve summoned the multitude of the disciples and said, "It is not desirable that we should leave the word of God and serve tables. Therefore, brethren, seek out from among you seven men of good reputation, full of the Holy Spirit and wisdom, whom we may appoint over this business; but we will give ourselves continually to prayer and to the ministry of the word." And the saying pleased the whole multitude. And they chose Stephen, a man full of faith and the Holy Spirit, and Philip, Prochorus, Nicanor, Timon, Parmenas, and Nicolas, a proselyte from Antioch, whom they set before the apostles; and when they had prayed, they laid hands on them. Then the word of God spread, and the number of the disciples multiplied greatly in Jerusalem, and a great many of the priests were obedient to the faith. And Stephen, full of faith and power, did great wonders and signs among the people. Then there arose some from what is called the Synagogue of the Freedmen (Cyrenians, Alexandrians, and those from Cilicia and Asia), disputing with Stephen. And they were not able to resist the wisdom and the Spirit by which he spoke. Then they secretly induced men to say, "We have heard him speak blasphemous words against Moses and God." And they stirred up the people, the elders, and the scribes; and they came upon him, seized him, and brought him to the council. They also set up false witnesses who said, "This man does not cease to speak blasphemous words against this holy place and the law; for we have heard him say that this Jesus of Nazareth will destroy this place and change the customs which Moses delivered to us." And all who sat in the council, looking steadfastly at him, saw his face as the face of an angel. Then the high priest said, "Are these things so?" And he said, "Brethren and fathers, listen....You stiffnecked and uncircumcised in heart and ears! You always resist the Holy Spirit; as your fathers did, so do you. Which of the prophets did your fathers not persecute? And they killed those who foretold the coming of the Just One, of whom you now have become the betrayers and murderers, who have received the law by the direction of angels and have not kept it." When they heard these things they were cut to the heart, and they gnashed at him with their teeth. But he, being full of the Holy Spirit, gazed into heaven and saw the glory of God, and Jesus standing at the right hand of God, and said, "Look! I see the heavens opened and the Son of Man standing at the right hand of God!" Then they cried out with a loud voice, stopped their

*ears, and ran at him with one accord; and they cast
him out of the city and stoned him. And the witnesses
laid down their clothes at the feet of a young man
named Saul. And they stoned Stephen as he was
calling on God and saying, "Lord Jesus, receive my
spirit." Then he knelt down and cried out with a loud
voice, "Lord, do not charge them with this sin." And
when he had said this, he fell asleep.*
—*Acts 6:1–7:2, 51–60*

 n the days when the number of disciples began to multiply, there arose a situation in which the Twelve had to make a definite decision not to occupy themselves with serving tables, but to give themselves continually to prayer and to the ministry of the Word. How important it is for all God's ministers to be continually in prayer and constantly feeding on the Scriptures of Truth. I often offer a reward to anyone who can catch me anywhere without my Bible or my New Testament.

None of you can be strong in God unless you are diligently and constantly listening to what God has to say to you through His Word. You cannot know the power and the nature of God unless you partake of His inbreathed Word. Read it in the morning, in the evening, and at every opportunity you get. After every meal, instead of indulging in unprofitable conversation around the table, read a chapter from the Word, and then have a season of prayer. I endeavor to make a point of doing this no matter where or with whom I am staying.

The psalmist said that he had hidden God's Word in his heart so that he might not sin against

Him (Ps. 119:11). You will find that the more of God's Word you hide in your heart, the easier it is to live a holy life. He also testified that God's Word had given him life (v. 50). As you receive God's Word, your whole physical being will be given life, and you will be made strong. As you receive with meekness the Word (James 1:21), you will find faith springing up within. You will have life through the Word.

A Better Plan for You

The Twelve told the rest of the disciples to find seven men to look after the business side of things. They were to be men with a good reputation and filled with the Holy Spirit. Those who were chosen were just ordinary men, but they were filled with the Holy Spirit, and this infilling always lifts a man to a plane above the ordinary. It does not take a cultured or an educated man to fill a position in God's church. What God requires is a yielded, consecrated, holy life, and He can make it a flame of fire. He can baptize *"with the Holy Spirit and fire"* (Matt. 3:11)!

The multitude chose seven men to serve tables. Undoubtedly, they were faithful in their appointed tasks, but we see that God soon had a better plan for two of them—Philip and Stephen. Philip was so full of the Holy Spirit that he could have a revival wherever God put him down. (See Acts 8:5–8, 26–40.) Man chose him to serve tables, but God chose him to win souls.

Oh, if I could only stir you up to see that, as you are faithful in the humblest role, God can fill you with His Spirit, make you a chosen vessel for Himself, and promote you to a place of mighty ministry in the salvation of souls and in the healing of the sick. Nothing is impossible to a man filled with the Holy Spirit. The possibilities are beyond all human comprehension. When you are filled with the power of the Holy Spirit, God will wonderfully work wherever you go.

When you are filled with the Spirit, you will know the voice of God. I want to give you one illustration of this. When I was going to Australia recently, our boat stopped at Aden and Bombay. In Aden the people came around the ship selling their wares—beautiful carpets and all sorts of Oriental things. There was one man selling some ostrich feathers. As I was looking over the side of the ship watching the trading, a gentleman said to me, "Would you join me in buying that bunch of feathers?" What did I want with feathers? I had no use for such things and no room for them either. But the gentleman asked me again, "Will you join me in buying that bunch?" The Spirit of God said to me, "Do it."

The feathers were sold to us for three pounds, and the gentleman said, "I have no money on me, but if you will pay the man for them, I will send the cash down to you by the steward." I paid for the feathers and gave the gentleman his share. He was traveling first class, and I was traveling second class. I said to him, "No, please don't give that money to the steward. I want you to bring it to me personally in my cabin." I asked the Lord, "What about these feathers?" He showed me that He had a purpose in my purchasing them.

A little while later, the gentleman came to my cabin and said, "I've brought the money." I said to him, "It is not your money that I want; it is your soul that I am seeking for God." Right there he opened up the whole story of his life and began to seek God, and that morning he wept his way through to God's salvation.

You have no idea what God can do through you when you are filled with His Spirit. Every day and every hour you can have the divine leading of God. To be filled with the Holy Spirit is great in every respect. I have seen some who had been suffering for years, but when they have been filled with the Holy Spirit, every bit of their sickness has passed away. The Spirit of God has made real to them the life of Jesus, and they have been completely liberated from every sickness and infirmity.

Look at Stephen. He was just an ordinary man chosen to serve tables. But the Holy Spirit was in him, and he was *"full of faith and power"* (Acts 6:8); therefore, he did great wonders and miracles among the people. There was no resisting *"the wisdom and the Spirit by which he spoke"* (v. 10). How important it is that every man be filled with the Holy Spirit.

> *An Interpretation of Tongues:* "The divine will is that you be filled with God, that the power of the Spirit fill you with the mightiness of God. There is nothing God will withhold from a man filled with the Holy Spirit."

I want to impress the importance of this upon you. It is not healing that I am presenting to you in these meetings—it is the living Christ. It is a glorious fact that the Son of God came down to bring *"liberty to the captives"* (Luke 4:18). He is the One who baptizes *"with the Holy Spirit and fire"* (Matt. 3:11). He is the One who is pouring forth what we are now seeing and hearing.

The Blessing of Persecution

How is it that the moment you are filled with the Holy Spirit persecution starts? It was so with the Lord Jesus Himself. We do not read of any persecution before the Holy Spirit came down upon Him like a dove. Shortly after this, we find that after He preached in His hometown, the people wanted to throw Him over the brow of a hill. (See Luke 4:16–30.) It was the same way with the twelve disciples. They had no persecution before the Day of Pentecost, but after they were filled with the Spirit, they were soon in prison. The Devil and the priests of religion will always get stirred when a man is filled with the Spirit and does things in the power of the Spirit. Nevertheless, persecution is the greatest blessing to a church. When we have persecution, we have purity. If you desire to be filled with the Spirit, you can count on one thing, and that is persecution. The Lord came to bring division (Luke 12:51), and even in your own household you may find *"three against two"* (v. 52).

The Lord Jesus gives us peace, but soon after you get peace within, you get persecution without. If you remain stationary, the Devil and his agents will not disturb you much. But when you press on and go the whole length with God, the Enemy has you as a target. But God will vindicate you in the midst of the whole thing.

At a meeting I was holding, the Lord was working, and many were being healed. A man saw what was taking place and remarked, "I'd like to try this thing." He came up for prayer and told me that his body was broken in two places. I laid my hands on him in the name of the Lord and said to him, "Now believe God." The next night he was at the meeting, and he got up like a lion. He said, "I want to tell you people that this man here is deceiving you. He laid his hands on me last night for a rupture in two places, but I'm not a bit better." I stopped him and said, "You are healed; your trouble is that you won't believe it."

He was at the meeting the next night, and when there was opportunity for testimonies, this man arose. He said, "I'm a mason by trade. Today I was working with a laborer, and he had to put a big stone in place. I helped him and did not feel any pain. I said to myself, 'How did I do that?' I went to a private place where I could take off my clothes, and I found that I was healed." I told the people, "Last night this man was against the Word of God, but now he believes it. It is true that *these signs will follow those who believe...they will lay hands on the sick, and they will recover'* (Mark 16:17–18). Healing is through the power that is in the name of Christ." It is the Spirit who has come to reveal the Word of God and to make it spirit and life to us (John 6:63).

Those of you who are seeking the baptism in the Holy Spirit are entering a place where you will have persecution. Your best friends will leave you—or those you may think are your best friends. No good friend will ever leave you. But be assured that your seeking is worthwhile. You will enter into a realm of illumination, a realm of revelation by the power of the Holy Spirit. He reveals the preciousness and the power of the blood of Christ. I find by the revelation of the Spirit that there is not one thing in me that the blood does not cleanse (1 John 1:9). I find that God sanctifies me by the blood and reveals the effectiveness of His work by the Spirit.

Life in the Spirit

Stephen was just an ordinary man, but he was clothed with the divine. He was *"full of faith and power"* (Acts 6:8), and great wonders and miracles were done by him. Oh, this life in the Holy Spirit! Oh, this life of deep inward revelation, of transformation from one state to another, of growing in grace, in all knowledge, and in the power of the Spirit. In this state, the life and the mind of Christ are renewed in you, and He gives constant revelations of the might of His power. It is only this kind of thing that will enable us to stand.

In this life, the Lord puts you in all sorts of places and then reveals His power. I had been preaching in New York, and one day I sailed for England on the *Lusitania*. As soon as I got on board, I went down to my cabin. Two men were there, and one of them said, "Well, will I do for company?" He took out a bottle and poured a glass of whiskey and drank it, and then he filled it up for me. "I never touch that stuff," I said. "How can you live without it?" he asked. "How could I live with it?" I asked. He admitted, "I have been under the influence of this stuff for months, and they say my insides are all shriveled up. I know that I am dying. I wish I could be delivered, but I just have to keep on drinking. Oh, if I could only be delivered! My father died in England

and has given me his fortune, but what good will it be to me except to hasten me to my grave?"

I said to this man, "Say the word, and you will be delivered." He asked, "What do you mean?" I said, "Say the word—show that you are willing to be delivered—and God will deliver you." But it was just as if I were talking to this platform for all the understanding he showed. I said to him, "Stand still," and I laid my hands on his head in the name of Jesus and cursed that alcohol demon that was taking his life. He cried out, "I'm free! I'm free! I know I'm free!" He took two bottles of whiskey and threw them overboard, and God saved, sobered, and healed him. I was preaching all the way across the ocean. He sat beside me at the table. Previous to this, he had not been able to eat, but now at every meal he went right through the menu.

You need only a touch from Jesus to have a good time. The power of God is just the same today. To me, He's lovely. To me, He's saving health. To me, He's the Lily of the Valley. Oh, this blessed Nazarene, this King of Kings! Hallelujah! Will you let Him have your will? Will you let Him have you? If so, all His power is at your disposal.

It's Worth It!

Those who disputed with Stephen *"were not able to resist the wisdom and the Spirit by which he spoke"* (Acts 6:10). Full of rage, they brought him to the council. However, God filled his face with a ray of heaven's light.

Being filled with the Spirit is worthwhile, no matter what it costs. Read in Acts 7 the mighty prophetic utterance by this holy man. Without fear he told them, *"You stiffnecked and uncircumcised in heart and ears! You always resist the Holy Spirit"* (Acts 7:51). When his enemies heard these things, *"they were cut to the heart"* (v. 54). There are two ways of being cut to the heart. Here they gnashed at him with their teeth, cast him out of the city, and stoned him. On the Day of Pentecost, when the people were cut to the heart, they cried out, *"What shall we do?"* (Acts 2:37). They responded in the opposite way. The Devil, if he can have his way, will cause you to commit murder. If Jesus has His way, you will repent.

Stephen, full of the Holy Spirit, looked up steadfastly into heaven and saw the glory of God and the Son of Man standing on the right hand of God. Oh, this being full of the Holy Spirit! How much it means! I was riding for sixty miles one summer day, and as I looked up at the heavens, I had an open vision of Jesus all the way. It takes the Holy Spirit to give this.

Stephen cried out, *"Lord, do not charge them with this sin"* (Acts 7:60). Since he was full of the Spirit, he was full of love. He manifested the very same compassion for his enemies that Jesus did at Calvary. This being filled with the Holy Spirit is great in every respect. It means constant filling and a new life continually. Oh, it's lovely! We have a wonderful Gospel and a great Savior! If you will only be filled with the Holy Spirit, you will have a constant spring within. Yes, as your faith centers on the Lord Jesus, from within you *"will flow rivers of living water"* (John 7:38).

Twenty-Two

Is Anyone Sick?

s there anyone sick? Is there anyone sick in this place?" This is what I ask when I go into a sickroom. Why? I will tell you a story that will explain.

My daughter is a missionary to Africa. I am interested in helping to support missionaries in Africa and all over. I love missionary work.

We had a missionary out in China who by some means or other got rheumatism. I have no word for rheumatism, only "devil-possessed." Rheumatism, cancer, tumors, lumbago, neuralgia—all these things I give only one name: the power of the Devil working in humanity. When I see tuberculosis, I see demon power working there. All these things can be removed.

When Jesus went into Peter's house, where his wife's mother lay sick, what did He do? Did He cover her up with a blanket and put a hot water bottle on her feet? If He didn't do that, why didn't He? Because He knew that the demons had all the heat of hell in them. He did the right thing: He rebuked the fever, and it left. (See Luke 4:38–39.) We, too, ought to do the right thing with these diseases.

Is Anyone Sick?

This missionary came home to Belfast from China, enraged against the work of God, enraged against God, enraged against everything. She was absolutely outside the plan of God.

While she was in Belfast, God allowed this missionary to fall down the steps and dislocate her backbone. Others had to lift her up and carry her to her bed. God allowed it.

Be careful about getting angry at God because of something wrong with your body. Get right with God.

On the day that I was to visit the sick, she asked me to come. When I went to her room, I looked at her and called out, "Is there anyone sick in this room?" No response. "Is there anyone sick in this room?" No response. "Well," I said, "we will wait until somebody moves."

By and by, she said, "Yes, I am sick." I said, "All right, we have found you out then. You are in the room. Now the Word of God says that when you are sick, you are to pray. When you pray, I will anoint you and pray for you, but not before."

It took her almost a quarter of an hour to yield, the Devil had such possession of her. But, thank God, she yielded. Then she cried and cried, and by the power of God her body was shaken loose, and she was set free. This happened when she repented, and not before.

Oh, what would happen if everybody in this place would repent! Talk about blessings! The glory would fall so you couldn't get out of this place. We need to see that God wants us to be blessed, but first of all He wants us to be ready for the blessing.

Believe and Be Healed

The God who told Moses to make a bronze serpent and put it on a pole so that whoever looked could be healed (see Numbers 21:5–9), now says, "The bronze serpent is not on the pole. Jesus is not on the cross. He has risen and has been given all power and authority. Believe. You will be healed if you believe."

You cannot literally look at the cross, you cannot literally look at the serpent, but you can believe. If you believe, you can be healed. God means for you to believe today; God means for you to be helped today.

Complete versus Partial Healing

I want everybody to know that Wigglesworth does not believe in partial healings. Then what does Wigglesworth believe? I believe in complete healings. If the healing is not manifested, it is there all the same. It is inactive because of inactive faith, but it is there. God has given it. How do I know? *"They will lay hands on the sick, and **they will recover**"* (Mark 16:18, emphasis added). Whose word is that? That is God's Word. So I have faith today. Hallelujah! Even repeating the Word gives me more faith.

> *An Interpretation of Tongues:* "Why do you doubt when God, even the Lord, has come to cast the Devil out, so that you may know that you are free from all things by the blood of Jesus?"

We are in a great place. The Lord is in the midst of us. You are to go away free today.

A Woman Sees a Vision

I like the thought, *"He Himself took our infirmities and bore our sicknesses"* (Matt. 8:17).

I want to tell you a remarkable story. One day I was standing at the bottom of Shanklin Road, Belfast, Ireland, with a piece of paper in my hand, looking at the addresses of where I had to go, when a man came over and said to me, "Are you visiting the sick?" "Yes," I said. "Go there," he said, and pointed to a house nearby.

I knocked at the door. No reply. I knocked again, and then a voice inside said, "Come in!" So I opened the door and walked in. Then a young man pointed for me to go up the stairway.

When I got up onto the landing, there was a door wide open. So I walked right through the doorway and found a woman sitting up on the bed. As soon as I looked at her, I knew she couldn't speak to me, so I began to pray. She was rocking back and forth, gasping for breath. I knew she was beyond answering me.

When I prayed, the Lord said to me—the Holy Spirit said distinctly—"Read Isaiah 53." So I opened the Book and began to read,

> *Who has believed our report? And to whom has the arm of the LORD been revealed? For He shall grow up before Him as a tender plant, and as a root out of dry ground.* (Isa. 53:1–2)

When I got to the fifth verse, *"But He was wounded for our transgressions, He was bruised for our iniquities; the chastisement for our peace was*

173

upon Him, and by His stripes we are healed," the woman shouted, "I am healed!"

"Oh!" I said. "Tell me what happened."

"Two weeks ago I was cleaning the house," she said. "In moving some furniture, I strained my heart; it moved out of its place. The doctors examined me and said that I would die of suffocation. But last night, in the middle of the night, I saw you come into the room. When you saw me, you knew I could not speak, so you began to pray. Then you opened to Isaiah 53 and read until you came to the fifth verse, and when you read the fifth verse, I was completely healed. That was a vision; now it is a fact."

So I know the Word of God is still true.

> *An Interpretation of Tongues:* "Stretch out your hand, for the Lord your God is so nigh unto you. He will take you and so place you in His pavilion of splendor that if you will not go out anymore but will remain stationary in the will of God, He will grant you the desire of your heart."

Now that is a word from the Lord. You will never get anything more distinct than that from the Lord. People miss the greatest plan of healing because of moving from one thing to another. Become stationary. God wants you to take the Word, claim the Word, and believe the Word. That is the perfect way of healing. Do not turn to the right hand or to the left (Deut. 5:32), but believe God.

God's Presence Heals

I believe we ought to have people in this meeting loosed from their infirmities even without having hands laid upon them. I see more and more that the day of the visitation of the Lord is upon us, that the presence of the Lord is here to heal. We should have people healed in these meetings while I am speaking, healed under the anointing of the Spirit.

I have been preaching faith so that you may definitely claim your healing. I believe that if you have listened to the Word and have been moved to believe, if you stand up while I pray, you will find that God's healing power will loose you from sickness.

> *An Interpretation of Tongues:* "In the depths God has come and moves, and moves in the very inner working of the heart until the Spirit of the Lord has perfect choice, and brings forth that which will resound to His glory forever. The Lord is in the midst of it. Those who are bound are made free from captivity."

God wants you to have a living faith now; He wants you to get a vital touch, shaking the foundation of all weakness. When you were saved, you were saved the moment you believed, and you will be healed the moment you believe.

Father, I take these people and present them to You, giving them into Your gracious, glorious care, so that You may keep them from falling, keep them from the error of the ways of the wicked, and deliver them from all evil. Let Your mercy be with them in their homes, in their bodies, and in every way. Amen.

Twenty-Three

Do You Want to Be Made Well?

believe the Word of God is so powerful that it can transform any and every life. There is power in God's Word to make that which does not exist to appear. There is executive power in the words that proceed from His lips. The psalmist told us, *"He sent His Word and healed them"* (Ps. 107:20). Do you think the Word has diminished in its power? I tell you, it has not. God's Word can bring things to pass today as it did in the past.

The psalmist said, *"Before I was afflicted I went astray, but now I keep Your word"* (Ps. 119:67). And again, *"It is good for me that I have been afflicted, that I may learn Your statutes"* (v. 71). If our afflictions will bring us to the place where we see that we cannot *"live by bread alone, but by every word that proceeds from the mouth of God"* (Matt. 4:4), they will have served a blessed purpose. I want you to realize that there is a life of purity, a life made clean through the Word He has spoken, in which, through faith, you can glorify God with a body that is free from sickness, as well as with a spirit set free from the bondage of Satan.

Around the pool of Bethesda lay a great multitude of sick folk—blind, lame, paralyzed—waiting for the moving of the water. (See John 5:2–4.) Did Jesus heal all of them? No, He left many around that pool unhealed. Undoubtedly, many had their eyes on the pool and had no eyes for Jesus. There are many today who always have their confidence in things they can see. If they would only get their eyes on God instead of on natural things, how quickly they would be helped.

The Bread of Healing

The following question arises: Is salvation and healing for all? It is for all who will press right in and claim their portion. Do you remember the case of that Syro-Phoenician woman who wanted the demon cast out of her daughter? Jesus said to her, *"Let the children be filled first, for it is not good to take the children's bread and throw it to the little dogs"* (Mark 7:27). Note that healing and deliverance are here spoken of by the Master as *"the children's bread"*; therefore, if you are a child of God, you can surely press in for your portion.

The Syro-Phoenician woman purposed to get from the Lord what she was after, and she said, *"Yes, Lord, yet even the little dogs under the table eat from the children's crumbs"* (v. 28). Jesus was stirred as He saw the faith of this woman, and He told her, *"For this saying go your way; the demon has gone out of your daughter"* (v. 29).

Today many children of God are refusing their blood-purchased portion of health in Christ and throwing it away. Meanwhile, sinners are pressing through and picking it up from under the table and are finding the cure, not only for their bodies, but also for their spirits and souls. The Syro-Phoenician woman went home and found that the demon had indeed gone out of her daughter. Today there is bread—there is life and health—for every child of God through His powerful Word.

The Word can drive every disease away from your body. Healing is your portion in Christ, who Himself is our bread, our life, our health, our All in All. Though you may be deep in sin, you can come to Him in repentance, and He will forgive and cleanse and heal you. His words are spirit and life to those who will receive them (John 6:63). There is a promise in the last verse of Joel that says, *"I will cleanse their blood that I have not cleansed"* (Joel 3:21 KJV). This as much as says that He will provide new life within. The life of Jesus Christ, God's Son, can so purify people's hearts and minds that they become entirely transformed—spirit, soul, and body.

The sick folk were around the pool of Bethesda, and one particular man had been there a long time. His infirmity was of thirty-eight years' standing. Now and again an opportunity to be healed would come as the angel stirred the waters, but he would be sick at heart as he saw another step in and be healed before him. Then one day Jesus was passing that way, and seeing him lying there in that sad condition, He asked, *"Do you want to be made well?"* (John 5:6). Jesus said it, and His words are from everlasting to everlasting. These are His words today to you, tried and tested one. You may say, like this poor sick man, "I have missed every opportunity up until now." Never mind that. *"Do you want to be made well?"*

Is It the Lord's Will?

I visited a woman who had been suffering for many years. She was all twisted up with rheumatism and had been in bed two years. I asked her, "What makes you lie here?" She said, "I've come to the conclusion that I have a thorn in the flesh." I said, "To what wonderful degree of righteousness have you attained that you must have a thorn in the flesh? Have you had such an abundance of divine revelations that there is a danger of your being exalted above measure?" (See 2 Corinthians 12:7–9.) She said, "I believe it is the Lord who is causing me to suffer." I said, "You believe it is the Lord's will for you to suffer, but you are trying to get out of it as quickly as you can. You have medicine bottles all over the place. Get out of your hiding place, and confess that you are a sinner. If you'll get rid of your self-righteousness, God will do something for you. Drop the idea that you are so holy that God has to afflict you. Sin is the cause of your sickness, not righteousness. Disease is not caused by righteousness, but by sin."

There is healing through the blood of Christ and deliverance for every captive. God never intended His children to live in misery because of some affliction that comes directly from the Devil. A perfect atonement was made at Calvary. I believe that Jesus

bore my sins, and I am free from them all. I am justified from all things if I dare to believe (Acts 13:39).
*"He Himself took our infirmities and bore our sick-
nesses"* (Matt. 8:17), and if I dare to believe, I can be
healed.

See this helpless man at the pool. Jesus asked
him, *"Do you want to be made well?"* (John 5:6). But
there was a difficulty in the way. The man had one
eye on the pool and one eye on Jesus. If you will look
only to Christ and put both of your eyes on Him, you
can be made every bit whole—spirit, soul, and body.
It is the promise of the living God that those who
believe are justified, made free, from all things (Acts
13:39). And *"if the Son makes you free, you shall be
free indeed"* (John 8:36).

You say, "Oh, if I could only believe!" Jesus understands. He knew that the helpless man had been
in that condition for a long time. He is full of compassion. He knows about that kidney trouble; He
knows about those corns; He knows about that neuralgia. There is nothing He does not know. He wants
only a chance to show Himself merciful and gracious
to you, but He wants to encourage you to believe
Him. If you can only believe, you can be saved and
healed. Dare to believe that Jesus was wounded for
your transgressions, was bruised for your iniquities,
was chastised that you might have peace, and that
by His stripes there is healing for you here and now
(Isa. 53:5). You have failed because you have not believed Him. Cry out to Him even now, *"Lord, I believe; help my unbelief!"* (Mark 9:24).

I was in Long Beach, California, one day. I was
with a friend, and we were passing by a hotel. He
told me of a doctor there who had a diseased leg. He

had been suffering from it for six years and could not get around. We went up to his room and found four doctors there. I said, "Well, doctor, I see you have plenty going on. I'll come again another day." I was passing by another time, and the Spirit said, "Go see him." Poor doctor! He surely was in poor shape. He said, "I have been like this for six years, and nobody can help me." I said, "You need almighty God." People are trying to patch up their lives, but they cannot do anything without God. I talked to him for a while about the Lord and then prayed for him. I cried, "Come out of him in the name of Jesus." The doctor cried, "It's all gone!"

Oh, if we only knew Jesus! One touch of His might meets the need of every crooked thing. The trouble is getting people to believe Him. The simplicity of this salvation is so wonderful. One touch of living faith in Him is all that is required for wholeness to be your portion.

I was in Long Beach about six weeks later, and the sick were coming for prayer. Among those filling up the aisle was the doctor. I said, "What is the trouble?" He said, "Diabetes, but it will be all right tonight. I know it will be all right." There is no such thing as the Lord's not meeting your need. There are no *if*s or *may*s; His promises are all *shall*s. *"All things are possible to him who believes"* (Mark 9:23). Oh, the name of Jesus! There is power in that name to meet every human need.

At that meeting there was an old man helping his son to the altar. He said, "He has fits—many every day." Then there was a woman with cancer. Oh, what sin has done! We read that when God brought forth His people from Egypt, *"there was not one feeble person among their tribes"* (Ps. 105:37 KJV). No disease! All healed by the power of God! I believe that God wants a people like that today.

I prayed for the woman who had the cancer, and she said, "I know I'm free and that God has delivered me." Then they brought the boy with the fits, and I commanded the evil spirits to leave in the name of Jesus. Then I prayed for the doctor. At the next night's meeting the house was full. I called out, "Now, doctor, what about the diabetes?" He said, "It is gone." Then I said to the old man, "What about your son?" He said, "He hasn't had any fits since." We have a God who answers prayer.

Sin and Sickness

Jesus meant this man at the pool to be a testimony forever. When he had both eyes on Jesus, He said to him, "Do the impossible thing. *'Rise, take up your bed and walk'* (John 5:8)." Jesus once called on a man with a withered hand to do the impossible—to stretch forth his hand. The man did the impossible thing. He stretched out his hand, and it was made completely whole. (See Matthew 12:10–13.)

In the same way, this helpless man began to rise, and he found the power of God moving within him. He wrapped up his bed and began to walk off. It was the Sabbath day, and there were some folks who, because they thought much more of a day than they did of the Lord, began to make a fuss. When the power of God is being manifested, a protest will always come from some hypocrites. Jesus knew all about what the man was going through and met him

182

again. This time He said to him, *"See, you have been made well. Sin no more, lest a worse thing come upon you"* (John 5:14).

There is a close relationship between sin and sickness. How many know that their sicknesses are a direct result of sin? I hope that no one will come to be prayed for who is living in sin. But if you will obey God and repent of your sin and stop it, God will meet you, and neither your sickness nor your sin will remain. *"The prayer of faith will save the sick, and the Lord will raise him up. And if he has committed sins, he will be forgiven"* (James 5:15).

Faith is just the open door through which the Lord comes. Do not say, "I was saved by faith" or "I was healed by faith." Faith does not save and heal. God saves and heals through that open door. You believe, and the power of Christ comes. Salvation and healing are for the glory of God. I am here because God healed me when I was dying, and I have been around the world preaching this full redemption, doing all I can to bring glory to the wonderful name of the One who healed me.

"Sin no more, lest a worse thing come upon you" (John 5:14). The Lord told us in one place about an evil spirit going out of a man. The house that the evil spirit left got all swept and put in order, but it received no new occupant. That evil spirit, with seven other spirits more wicked than himself, went back to that unoccupied house, and *"the last state of that man* [was] *worse than the first"* (Matt. 12:45).

The Lord does not heal you to go to a baseball game or to a racetrack. He heals you for His glory so that from that moment your life will glorify Him. But this man remained stationary. He did not magnify

God. He did not seek to be filled with the Spirit. And his last state became *"worse than the first."*

The Lord wants to so cleanse the motives and desires of our hearts that we will seek one thing only, and that is His glory. I went to a certain place one day and the Lord said, "This is for My glory." A young man had been sick for a long time. He had been confined to his bed in an utterly hopeless condition. He was fed with a spoon and was never dressed. The weather was damp, so I said to the people in the house, "I wish you would put the young man's clothes by the fire to air." At first they would not take any notice of my request, but because I was persistent, they at last got out his clothes. When they had been aired, I took them into his room.

The Lord said to me, "You will have nothing to do with this," and I just lay prostrate on the floor. The Lord showed me that He was going to shake the place with His glory. The very bed shook. I laid my hands on the young man in the name of Jesus, and the power fell in such a way that I fell with my face to the floor. In about a quarter of an hour, the young man got up and walked back and forth praising God. He dressed himself and then went out to the room where his father and mother were. He said, "God has healed me." Both the father and mother fell prostrate to the floor as the power of God surged through that room. There was a woman in that house who had been in an asylum for lunacy, and her condition was so bad that they were about to take her back. But the power of God healed her, too.

The power of God is just the same today as it was in the past. Men need to be taken back to the old paths, to the old-time faith, to believing God's

Word and every "Thus says the Lord" in it. The Spirit of the Lord is moving in these days. God is coming forth. If you want to be in the rising tide, you must accept all God has said.

"Do you want to be made well?" (John 5:6). It is Jesus who asks this question. Give Him your answer. He will hear, and He will answer.

Twenty-Four

The Words of This Life

But a certain man named Ananias, with Sapphira his wife, sold a possession. And he kept back part of the proceeds, his wife also being aware of it, and brought a certain part and laid it at the apostles' feet. But Peter said, "Ananias, why has Satan filled your heart to lie to the Holy Spirit and keep back part of the price of the land for yourself? While it remained, was it not your own? And after it was sold, was it not in your own control? Why have you conceived this thing in your heart? You have not lied to men but to God." Then Ananias, hearing these words, fell down and breathed his last. So great fear came upon all those who heard these things. And the young men arose and wrapped him up, carried him out, and buried him. Now it was about three hours later when his wife came in, not knowing what had happened. And Peter answered her, "Tell me whether you sold the land for so much?" She said, "Yes, for so much." Then Peter said to her, "How is it that you have agreed together to test the Spirit of the Lord? Look, the feet of those who have buried your husband are at the door, and they will carry you out." Then

immediately she fell down at his feet and breathed her last. And the young men came in and found her dead, and carrying her out, buried her by her husband. So great fear came upon all the church and upon all who heard these things. And through the hands of the apostles many signs and wonders were done among the people. And they were all with one accord in Solomon's Porch. Yet none of the rest dared join them, but the people esteemed them highly. And believers were increasingly added to the Lord, multitudes of both men and women, so that they brought the sick out into the streets and laid them on beds and couches, that at least the shadow of Peter passing by might fall on some of them. Also a multitude gathered from the surrounding cities to Jerusalem, bringing sick people and those who were tormented by unclean spirits, and they were all healed. Then the high priest rose up, and all those who were with him (which is the sect of the Sadducees), and they were filled with indignation, and laid their hands on the apostles and put them in the common prison. But at night an angel of the Lord opened the prison doors and brought them out, and said, "Go, stand in the temple and speak to the people all the words of this life."
—*Acts 5:1–20*

Notice this expression that the Lord gives of the gospel message—*"the words of this life."* It is the most wonderful life possible—the life of faith in the Son of God. This is the life where God is present all the time. He is all around, and He is within. It is the life of many revelations and of many manifestations of God's

Holy Spirit, a life in which the Lord is continually seen, known, felt, and heard. It is a life without death, for *"we have passed from death to life"* (1 John 3:14). The very life of God has come within us. Where that life is in its fullness, disease cannot exist. It would take me a month to tell what there is in this wonderful life. Everyone can enter in and possess and be possessed by this life.

It is possible for you to be within the vicinity of this life and yet miss it. It is possible for you to be in a place where God is pouring out His Spirit and yet miss the blessing that God is so willing to bestow. This is all due to a lack of revelation and a misunderstanding of the infinite grace of God and of *"the God of all grace"* (1 Pet. 5:10), who is willing to give to all who will reach out the hand of faith. This life that He freely bestows is a gift. Some think they have to earn it, and they miss the whole thing. Oh, for a simple faith to receive all that God so lavishly offers! You can never be ordinary from the day you receive this life from above. You become extraordinary, filled with the extraordinary power of our extraordinary God.

Why Did Ananias and Sapphira Die?

Ananias and Sapphira were in the wonderful revival that God gave to the early church, yet they missed it. They thought that possibly the thing might fail. They wanted to have a reserve for themselves in case it turned out to be a failure.

There are many people like them today. Many people make vows to God in times of great crisis in their lives but fail to keep their vows, and in the end they become spiritually bankrupt. Blessed is the man *"who swears to his own hurt and does not change"* (Ps. 15:4), who keeps the vow he has made to God, who is willing to lay his all at God's feet. The man who does this never becomes a lean soul. God has promised to *"strengthen* [his] *bones"* (Isa. 58:11). There is no dry place for such a man. He is always *"fresh and flourishing"* (Ps. 92:14), and he becomes stronger and stronger. It pays to trust God with all and to hold back nothing.

I wish I could make you see how great a God we have. Ananias and Sapphira were really doubting God and were questioning whether this work that He had begun would go on. They wanted to get some glory for selling their property, but because of their lack of faith, they kept part of the proceeds in reserve in case the work of God were to fail.

Many are doubting whether this Pentecostal revival will go on. Do you think this Pentecostal work will stop? Never. For fifteen years I have been in constant revival, and I am sure that it will never stop. When George Stephenson built his first engine, he took his sister Mary to see it. She looked at it and said to her brother, "George, it'll never go." He said to her, "Get in, Mary." She said again, "It'll never go." He said to her, "We'll see; you get in." Mary at last got in. The whistle blew, there was a puff and a rattle, and the engine started off. Then Mary cried out, "George, it'll never stop! It'll never stop!"

People are looking at this Pentecostal revival, and they are very critical. They are saying, "It'll never go." However, when they are induced to come into the work, they one and all say, "It'll never stop." This revival of God is sweeping on and on, and there is no stopping the current of life, of love, of inspiration, and of power.

> *An Interpretation of Tongues:* "It is the living Word who has brought this. It is the Lamb in the midst, 'the same yesterday, today, and forever.'"

God has brought unlimited resources for everyone. Do not doubt. Hear with the ear of faith. God is in the midst. See that it is God who has set forth what you see and hear today (Acts 2:33).

I want you to see that in the early church, controlled by the power of the Holy Spirit, it was not possible for a lie to exist. The moment it came into the church, there was instant death. And as the power of the Holy Spirit increases in these days of the latter rain, it will be impossible for any man to remain in our midst with a lying spirit. God will purify the church. The Word of God will be in such power in healing and other spiritual manifestations, that great fear will be upon all those who see these things.

To the natural mind, it seems a small thing for Ananias and Sapphira to want to have a little to fall back on, but I want to tell you that you can please God and get things from God only through a living faith. God never fails. God never can fail.

Our Merciful and Healing God

When I was in Bergen, Norway, there came to the meeting a young woman who was employed at the hospital as a nurse. A big cancerous tumor had developed on her nose. The nose was enlarged and had become black and very inflamed. She came for prayer, and I asked her, "What is your condition?" She said, "I dare not touch my nose; it gives me so much pain." I said to all the people, "I want you to look at this nurse and notice her terrible condition. I believe that our God is merciful, that He is faithful, and that He will bring to nothing this condition that the Devil has brought about. I am going to curse this disease in the all-powerful name of Jesus. The pain will go. I believe God will give us an exhibition of His grace, and I will ask this young woman to come to the meeting tomorrow night and declare what God has done for her."

Oh, the awfulness of sin! Oh, the awfulness of the power of sin! Oh, the awfulness of the consequences of the Fall! When I see a cancerous tumor, I ask, "Can this be the work of God?" God help me to show you that this is the work of the Devil, and to show you the way out.

I do not condemn people who sin. I don't scold people. I know what is behind the sin. I know that Satan is always going about *"like a roaring lion, seeking whom he may devour"* (1 Pet. 5:8). I always remember the patience and love of the Lord Jesus Christ. When they brought to Him a woman whom they had taken in adultery, telling Him that they had caught her in the very act, He simply stooped down and wrote on the ground. Then He quietly said, *"He who is without sin among you, let him throw a stone at her first"* (John 8:7). I have never seen a man without sin. *"All have sinned and fall short of the glory of God"* (Rom. 3:23). But I read in this blessed gospel message that God *"has laid on Him* [Jesus] *the iniquity of us all"* (Isa. 53:6).

When I see an evil condition, I feel that I must stand in my position and rebuke the condition. I laid my hands on the nose of that suffering nurse and cursed the evil power that was causing her so much distress. The next night the place was packed. The people were so jammed together that it seemed as if there was not room for one more to enter that house. How God's rain fell upon us! How good God is, so full of grace and so full of love. I saw the nurse in the audience and cried out, "Here's the woman whose nose I prayed for!" I asked her to come forward, and she came and showed everyone what God had done. He had perfectly healed her. Oh, I tell you, He is just the same Jesus. He is just the same today (Heb. 13:8). All things are possible if you dare to trust God (Mark 9:23).

Church Growth and Numerous Healings

When the power of God came so mightily upon the early church, even in the death of Ananias and Sapphira, great fear came upon all the people. And when we are in the presence of God, when God is working mightily in our midst, there comes a great fear, a reverence, a holiness of life, a purity that fears to displease God. We read that no man dared to join them, but God added to the church those who were being saved. I would rather have God add to our Pentecostal church than have all the town join it. God added daily to His own church.

The next thing that happened was that people became so assured that God was working that they knew that anything would be possible, and they brought their sick into the streets and laid them on beds and mats so that at least the shadow of Peter passing by might fall on them. Multitudes of sick people and those oppressed with evil spirits were brought to the apostles, and God healed every one of them. I do not believe that it was the shadow of Peter that healed them, but the power of God was mightily present, and the faith of the people was so aroused that they joined with one heart to believe God. God will always meet people on the basis of faith.

Revivals in Norway and Ireland

God's tide is rising all over the earth. I had been preaching in Stavanger, Norway, and was very tired and wanted a few hours' rest. I went to my next appointment, arriving at about 9:30 in the morning. My first meeting was to be at night. I said to my interpreter, "After we have had something to eat, let's go down to the sea." We spent three or four hours down by the sea and at about 4:30 returned. We found the end of the street, which had a narrow entrance, just filled with automobiles, wagons, and so on, containing invalids and sick people of every kind. I went up to the house and was told that the house was full of sick people, too. It reminded me of the scene that we read of in the fifth chapter of Acts. I began praying for the people in the street, and God began to heal the people. And how wonderfully He healed those people who were in the house! When we sat down to eat, the telephone rang, and someone at the other end was saying, "What are we going to do? The town hall is already full; the police cannot control things."

Beloved, the tide is rising; the fields are ripe for harvest (John 4:35). God gave us a wonderful revival. I want to be in a mighty revival. I was in one mighty revival in Wales, and I long to be in a great revival that will eclipse anything we have ever thought of. I have faith to believe it is coming.

In that little Norwegian town the people were jammed together, and oh, how the power of God fell upon us! A cry went up from everyone, "Isn't this the revival?" Revival is coming. The breath of the Almighty is coming. The breath of God shows every defect, and as it comes flowing in like a river, everybody will need a fresh anointing, a fresh cleansing of the blood. You can depend on it that that breath is upon us.

One time I was at a meeting in Ireland. There were many sick carried to that meeting, and helpless ones were brought there. Many people in that place were seeking the baptism in the Holy Spirit. Some of them had been seeking for years. There were sinners there who were under mighty conviction. A moment came when the breath of God swept through the meeting. In about ten minutes every sinner in the place was saved. Everyone who had been seeking the Holy Spirit was baptized, and every sick one was healed. God is a reality, and His power can never fail. As our faith reaches out, God will meet us, and the same rain will fall. It is the same blood that cleanses, the same power, the same Holy Spirit, and the same Jesus made real through the power of the Holy Spirit! What would happen if we would believe God?

The precious blood of the Lord Jesus Christ is effective; right now it will cleanse your heart and put this life, this wonderful life of God, within you. The blood will make you every bit whole if you dare to believe. The healing power of the blessed Son of God is right here for you, but so few will touch Him. The Bible is full of entreaty for you to come and partake and receive the grace, the power, the strength, the righteousness, and the full redemption of Jesus Christ. He never fails to hear when we believe. This same Jesus is in our midst to touch and to free you.

A Lame Man and His Son

One place where I was, a lame man was brought to me who had been in bed for two years, with no hope of recovery. He was brought thirty miles to the meeting, and he came up on crutches to be prayed for. His boy was also afflicted in the knees, and they had four crutches between the two of them. The man's face was full of torture. But there is healing power in the Lord, and He never fails to heal when we believe. In the name of Jesus—that name so full of power—I put my hand down that leg that was so diseased. The man threw down his crutches, and all were astonished as they saw him walking up and down without aid. The little boy called out to his father, "Papa, me; papa, me, me, me!" The little boy who had two withered knees wanted the same touch. And the same Jesus was there to bring a real deliverance to the little captive. He was completely healed.

These were legs that were touched. If God will stretch out His mighty power to loose afflicted legs, what mercy will He extend to that soul of yours that must exist forever? Hear the Lord say,

The Spirit of the LORD is upon Me, because He has anointed Me to preach the gospel to the poor; He has sent Me to heal the broken-hearted, to proclaim liberty to the captives and recovery of sight to the blind, to set at liberty those who are oppressed.   *(Luke 4:18)*

He invites you, *"Come to Me, all you who labor and are heavy laden, and I will give you rest"* (Matt. 11:28). God is willing in His great mercy to touch your limbs with His mighty power, and if He is willing to do this, how much more eager He is to deliver you from the power of Satan and to make you a child of the King! How much more necessary it is for you to be healed of your soul sickness than of your bodily ailments! And God is willing to give the double cure.

A Young Man Who Had Fallen into Sin

I was passing through the city of London one time, and Mr. Mundell, the secretary of the Pentecostal Missionary Union, found out that I was there. He arranged for me to meet him at a certain place at 3:30 in the afternoon. I was to meet a certain boy whose father and mother lived in the city of Salisbury. They had sent this young man to London to take care of their business. He had been a leader in Sunday school work, but he had been betrayed and had fallen. Sin is awful, and *"the wages of sin is death"* (Rom. 6:23). But there is another side—*"the gift of God is eternal life"* (v. 23).

This young man was in great distress; he had contracted a horrible disease and was afraid to tell anyone. There was nothing but death ahead for him. When the father and mother found out about his condition, they suffered inexpressible grief.

When we got to the house, Brother Mundell suggested that we begin to pray. I said, "God does not say so. We are not going to pray yet. I want to quote a Scripture: *'Fools, because of their transgression, and because of their iniquities, were afflicted. Their soul abhorred all manner of food, and they drew near to the gates of death'* (Ps. 107:17)." The young man cried out, "I am that fool." He broke down and told us the story of his fall. Oh, if men would only repent and confess their sins, how God would stretch out His hand to heal and to save! The moment that young man repented, a great abscess burst, and God sent power into that young man's life, giving him a mighty deliverance.

God is gracious and is *"not willing that any should perish"* (2 Pet. 3:9). How many are willing to make a clean break from their sins? I tell you that the moment you do this, God will open heaven. It is an easy thing for Him to save your soul and heal your disease if you will only come and take shelter today in *"the secret place of the Most High"* (Ps. 91:1). He will satisfy you with a long life and show you His salvation (v. 16). *"In [His] presence is fullness of joy; at [His] right hand are pleasures forevermore"* (Ps. 16:11). There is full redemption for all through the precious blood of the Son of God.

Twenty-Five

The Active Life of the Spirit-Filled Believer

hese are the last days, the days of the falling away. These are days when Satan is having a great deal of power. But we must keep in mind that Satan has no power except as he is allowed.

It is a great thing to know that God is loosing you from the world, loosing you from a thousand things. You must seek to have the mind of God in all things. If you don't, you will stop His working.

We will never know the mind of God until we learn to know the voice of God. The striking thing about Moses is that it took him forty years to learn human wisdom, forty years to know his helplessness, and forty years to live in the power of God. It took one hundred and twenty years to teach that man, and sometimes it seems to me that it will take many years to bring us to the place where we can discern the voice of God, the leadings of God, and all His will concerning us.

I see that all revelation, all illumination, everything that God had in Christ was to be brought forth into perfect light so that we might be able to live the same way, produce the same things, and in every activity be children of God with power. It must be so. We must not limit the Holy One. And we must clearly see that God brought us forth to make us supernatural, so that we might be changed all the time along the lines of the supernatural, so that we may every day so live in the Spirit that all of the revelations of God are just like a canvas thrown before our eyes, on which we see clearly step by step all the divine will of God.

Free in the Spirit

Any assembly that puts its hand on the working of the Spirit will surely dry up. The assembly must be as free in the Spirit as possible, and you must allow a certain amount of extravagance when people are getting through to God. Unless we are very wise, we can easily interfere with and quench the power of God that is upon us. It is an evident fact that one man in a meeting, filled with unbelief, can make a place for the Devil to have a seat. And it is very true that if we are not careful, we may quench the spirit of some person who is innocent but incapable of helping himself. *"We then that are strong ought to bear the infirmities of the weak"* (Rom. 15:1 KJV). If you want an assembly full of life, you must have one in which the Spirit of God is manifested. And in order to keep at the boiling point of that blessed incarnation of the Spirit, you must be as simple as babes;

you must be *"wise as serpents and harmless as doves"* (Matt. 10:16).

I always ask God for a leading of grace. It takes grace to be in a meeting because it is so easy, if you are not careful, to get on the natural side. If the preacher has lost the anointing, he will be well repaid if he will repent and get right with God and get the anointing back. It never pays to be less than spiritual. We must have a divine language, and the language must be of God. Beloved, if you come into perfect line with the grace of God, one thing will certainly take place in your life. You will change from that old position of the world where you are judging everybody and not trusting anybody, and you will come into a place where you will have a heart that will believe all things, a heart that under no circumstances retaliates when you are insulted.

The Sweet Touch of Heaven

I know many of you think many times before you speak once. Here is a great word: *"For your obedience has become known to all. Therefore I am glad on your behalf; but I want you to be wise in what is good, and simple concerning evil"* (Rom. 16:19). Innocent. No inward corruption or defilement, that is, not full of distrust, but just a holy, divine likeness of Jesus that dares believe that almighty God will surely watch over all. Hallelujah! *"No evil shall befall you, nor shall any plague come near your dwelling. For He shall give His angels charge over you, to keep you in all your ways"* (Ps. 91:10–11). The child of God who is rocked in the bosom of the Father has the sweetest touch of heaven, and the honey of the Word is always in his life.

If the saints only knew how precious they are in the sight of God (Isa. 43:4), they would scarcely be able to sleep for thinking of His watchful, loving care. Oh, He is a precious Jesus! He is a lovely Savior! He is divine in all His attitudes toward us, and He makes our hearts burn. There is nothing like it. "Oh," said the two men who had traveled to Emmaus with Jesus, "didn't our hearts burn within us as He walked with us and talked with us?" (See Luke 24:32.) Oh, beloved, it must be so today.

Always keep in mind the fact that the Holy Spirit must bring manifestation. We must understand that the Holy Spirit is breath, the Holy Spirit is a person, and it is the most marvelous thing to me to know that this Holy Spirit power can be in every part of our bodies. You can feel it from the crown of your head to the soles of your feet. Oh, it is lovely to be burning all over with the Holy Spirit! And when that takes place, the tongue must give forth the glory and the praise.

You must be in the place of magnifying the Lord. The Holy Spirit is the great Magnifier of Jesus, the great Illuminator of Jesus. After the Holy Spirit comes in, it is impossible to keep your tongue still. Why, you would burst if you didn't give Him utterance! What about a silent baptized soul? Such a person is not to be found in the Scriptures. You will find that when you speak to God in the new tongue He gives you, you enter into a close communion with Him never experienced before. Talk about preaching! I would like to know how it will be possible for all the people filled with the Holy Spirit to stop preaching. Even the sons and daughters must prophesy (Joel 2:28). After the Holy Spirit comes in, a man is in a new order in God. You will find it so real that you will want to sing, talk, laugh, and shout. We are in a strange place when the Holy Spirit comes in.

If the incoming of the Spirit is lovely, what must be the outflow? The incoming is only to be an outflow.

I am very interested in scenery. When I was in Switzerland, I wasn't satisfied until I went to the top of the mountain, though I like the valleys also. On the summit of the mountain, the sun beats on the snow and sends the water trickling down the mountain right through to the meadows. Go there and see if you can stop the water. It is the same way in the spiritual realm. God begins with the divine flow of His eternal power, which is the Holy Spirit, and you cannot stop it.

Spiritual Giants

We must always clearly see that the baptism in the Spirit must make us ministering spirits.

Peter and John had been baptized only a short time when they met the lame man at the temple. Did they know what they had? No. I challenge you to try to know what you have. No one knows what he has in the baptism in the Holy Spirit. You have no conception of it. You cannot measure it by any human standards. It is greater than any man can imagine; consequently, those two disciples had no idea what they had. For the first time after they had been baptized in the Holy Spirit, they came down to the Gate Beautiful. There they saw the man sitting who had been lame for over forty years. What was the first thing that happened after they saw him? Ministry. What was the second? Operation. What was the third? Manifestation, of course. It could not be otherwise. You will always find that this order in the Scriptures will be carried out in everybody.

I clearly see that we ought to have spiritual giants in the earth, mighty in understanding, amazing in activity, always having a wonderful testimony because of their faith-filled activity. I find instead that there are many people who perhaps have better discernment than the average believer, better knowledge of the Word than the average believer, but they have failed to put their discernment and knowledge into practice, so the gifts lie dormant. I am here to help you to begin doing mighty acts in the power of God through the gifts of the Spirit. You will find that what I am speaking on is from personal knowledge derived from wonderful experiences in many lands. The man who is filled with the Holy Spirit is always acting. The first verse of the Acts of the Apostles says, *"Jesus began both to do and teach."* Jesus had to begin to do, and so must we.

Help for the Suffering

Beloved, we must see that the baptism in the Holy Spirit is an activity with an outward manifestation. When I was in Norway, God was mightily moving there, though I had to talk through an interpreter. God always worked in a wonderful way. One day we met a man who stopped the three men I was with, one being the interpreter. I was walking on, but I saw he was in a dilemma, so I turned back and said to the interpreter, "What is the trouble?" "This man," he said, "is so full of neuralgia that he is almost blind, and he is in a terrible state." Just as soon as they finished the conversation, I said to the spirit that was afflicting him, "Come out of him in the name of Jesus." And the man said, "It is all gone! It is all gone! I am free." Ah, beloved, we have no conception of what God has for us!

I will tell you what happened in Sydney, Australia. A man with a cane passed by a friend and me. He had to get down and then twist over, and the torture on his face made a deep impression on my soul. I asked myself, "Is it right to pass by this man?" So I said to my friend, "There is a man in awful distress, and I cannot go farther. I must speak to him." I went over to this man and said to him, "You seem to be in great trouble." "Yes," he said, "I am no good and never will be." I said, "You see that hotel? Be in front of that door in five minutes, and I will pray for you, and you will be able to stand as straight as any man here." This is along the lines of activity in the faith of Jesus.

I came back after paying a bill, and he was there. I will never forget him wondering if he was going to be trapped, or why a man would stop him on the street and tell him he would be made to stand straight. However, I had said it, so it had to be. If you say anything, you must stand with God to make it so. Never say anything for bravado, unless you have the right to say it. Always be sure of your ground, and be sure that you are honoring God. If there is anything about the situation that will make *you* anything, it will bring you sorrow. Your whole ministry has to be along the lines of grace and blessing.

We helped him up the two steps, took him to the elevator, and got him upstairs. It was difficult to get him from the elevator to my room, as though Satan was making the last attempt for his life, but we got him there. In five minutes' time this man walked out of that room with his body as straight as any man's in this place. He walked perfectly and declared he hadn't a pain in his body.

Oh, beloved, it is ministry; it is operation; it is manifestation! Those are three of the leading principles of the baptism in the Holy Spirit. And we must see to it that God is producing these three through us.

The Bible is the Word of God. It has the truths, and whatever people may say of them, they stand stationary, unmovable. Not one word of all His good promises will fail (1 Kings 8:56). His Word will come forth. In heaven it is settled (Ps. 119:89). On earth the fact must be made manifest that He is the God of everlasting power.

Begin to Act

God wants manifestation, and He wants His glory to be seen. He wants us all to be filled with the thought that He can look upon us and delight in us subduing the world unto Him. You are going to miss a great deal if you don't begin to act. But once you begin to act in the order of God, you will find that God establishes your faith and from that day starts you along the line of the promises. When will you begin?

In a place in England, I was speaking about faith and what would take place if we believed God. Many things happened. When I left that place, it appeared that one man who worked in the coal mine had heard me. He had trouble with a stiff knee. He said to his wife, "I cannot help but think every day that that message of Wigglesworth's was to stir us to do something. I cannot get away from it. All the men in the pit know how I walk with a stiff knee, and you know how you have wrapped it with yards of flannel. Well, I am going to act. You have to be the congregation." He got his wife in front of him. "I am going to act and do just as Wigglesworth did." He got hold of his leg unmercifully, saying, "Come out, you devils; come out in the name of Jesus! Now, Jesus, help me. Come out, you devils; come out." Then he said, "Wife, they are gone! They are gone! This is too good. I am going to act now." So he went to his place of worship, and all the coal miners were there. It was a prayer meeting. As he told them this story, these men became delighted. They said, "Jack, come over here and help me." And Jack went. As soon as he was through in one home, he was invited to another, loosing these people from the pains they had gotten in the coal mine.

Ah, brothers and sisters, we have no idea what God has for us if we will only begin! But, oh, the grace we need! We may make a mistake. If you do this work outside of Him, if you do it for yourself, and if you want to be someone, it will be a failure. We will be able to succeed only as we do the work in the name of Jesus. Oh, the love that God's Son can put into us if we are only humble enough, weak enough, and helpless enough to know that unless He does it, it will not be done! *"Whatever things you ask when you pray, believe that you receive them, and you will have them"* (Mark 11:24).

Live in the Spirit. Walk in the Spirit. Walk in communion with the Spirit. Talk with God. All leadings of the divine order are for you. I pray that if there are any who have turned to their own way and have made God second, they will come to repentance. Let go of what is earthly, and take hold of God's ideals. God will bring you to an end of yourself. Begin with God this moment.